T0329153

Cambridge Elements ≡

Elements in Religion and Monotheism
edited by
Paul K. Moser
Loyola University Chicago
Chad Meister
Bethel University

MONOTHEISM AND FORGIVENESS

S. Mark Heim
Andover Newton Seminary at Yale Divinity School

CAMBRIDGE
UNIVERSITY PRESS

CAMBRIDGE
UNIVERSITY PRESS

University Printing House, Cambridge CB2 8BS, United Kingdom

One Liberty Plaza, 20th Floor, New York, NY 10006, USA

477 Williamstown Road, Port Melbourne, VIC 3207, Australia

314–321, 3rd Floor, Plot 3, Splendor Forum, Jasola District Centre,
New Delhi – 110025, India

103 Penang Road, #05–06/07, Visioncrest Commercial, Singapore 238467

Cambridge University Press is part of the University of Cambridge.

It furthers the University's mission by disseminating knowledge in the pursuit of
education, learning, and research at the highest international levels of excellence.

www.cambridge.org
Information on this title: www.cambridge.org/9781108737746
DOI: 10.1017/9781108642682

First published 2022

A catalogue record for this publication is available from the British Library.

ISBN 978-1-108-73774-6 Paperback
ISSN 2631-3014 (online)
ISSN 2631-3006 (print)

Monotheism and Forgiveness

Elements in Religion and Monotheism

DOI: 10.1017/9781108642682
First published online: February 2022

S. Mark Heim
Andover Newton Seminary at Yale Divinity School

Author for correspondence: S. Mark Heim, mark.heim@yale.edu

Abstract: Forgiveness is a hallmark teaching within monotheistic religions. This Element introduces the topic in three ways. First, it considers the extent to which forgiveness is specific to or constituted by monotheistic beliefs, by comparison with analogous teaching and practice in Buddhism. Second, the most extensive section explores the grammar of forgiveness shared across the Abrahamic traditions of Judaism, Christianity, and Islam – elements of repentance, intercession, and eschatological deferral. This section identifies some of the divergent tendencies or emphases on this topic among those traditions. The third section addresses the role of forgiveness and monotheistic religions in human cultural evolution and the emergence of eusociality. The aim is to provide the reader with an introductory view of monotheism and forgiveness from a comparative religious example, from an internal examination of Abrahamic traditions, and from a developmental, secular perspective.

Keywords: forgiveness, monotheism, comparative, theology, mercy

ISBNs: 9781108737746 (PB), 9781108642682 (OC)
ISSNs: 2631-3014 (online), 2631-3006 (print)

Contents

Introduction

Monotheistic religions affirm forgiveness as an assumption and an aspiration. The need for forgiveness in relation to the divine, and for persons and groups in relation to each other, appears to be a common axiom of revelation. Each monotheistic tradition encompasses rituals and practices related to forgiveness, as well as teachings that commend and explore it.[1] It may loom larger in the self-presentation of Christianity – such that even the title of this Element might suggest to some a Christian emphasis – but moving examples and commendations of it will be found equally in all.

What Is Forgiveness?

Forgiveness is the decision not to return evil for evil. We most readily understand forgiveness in the context of two parties: offender and offended or perpetrator and victim. Forgiveness is exercised by the injured party by forgoing punishment or just recompensing for an evil done to them. There is a proactive form of forgiveness in the choice not to insist on the exercise of a legitimate obligation owed by another (as in forgiving a debt). Here, no original injury is passed over. Instead, a relative "injury" is created by giving up what one is justly due. In either case, one disregards another person's past negative behavior or positive obligation, acting in important ways as if it had not happened. Forgiveness is a revision in the meaning of the past. Forgiveness in this sense is a course of action, a choice against retaliation. There are further reaches of forgiveness that involve a change in attitude toward the offenses and toward the offender, an internal change in the one forgiving. This can mean giving up negative emotions of anger and bitterness about the offense and/or the cultivation of positive emotions of empathy and compassion toward the offender. In a broader sense, forgiveness includes also the mirror image of this transformation on the part of the offender. Thus, there are actions on the part of a penitent to express regret, to request mercy, and to make restitution. There may be internal changes on their part: giving up the subjective dispositions that rationalize and defend the behavior involved, and cultivating empathy and compassion toward the one who has been harmed. Forgiveness in this sense is not only something extended as a gift but also something actively received.

Forgiveness can refer then not just to a change in the actions of or the internal dispositions within individuals but also to a change in the relation between them, a new condition of reconciliation that they share and that characterizes

---

[1] We can think of penitential practices of confession and repentance in Christian churches, the fasting and self-examination that attend Yom Kippur in Judaism, and similar features of Ramadan for all Muslims and of the Haj for those who perform it.

their continuing life in the future. Finally, we can look beyond forgiveness as a relation with only two sides, to consider its implications in the life of a community. In the house of monotheism, forgiveness is always at least a three-party problem. Any reconciliation of an individual with God implies changed behavior toward others; any human-to-human forgiveness involves God.

To summarize, forgiveness can mean:

1. the voluntary deferral of retaliatory punishment or justly owed benefits by one person in favor of another;
2. the internal psychic or spiritual healing of anger, pain, and guilt occasioned by injury – the inner dimension of giving and receiving pardon;
3. the condition of reconciliation that may result among the affected parties in (a) and (b);
4. non-retaliation as a feature of the function of communities or groups with regard to violations of its norms of justice by individuals within them, transgressions between members of the group, or between members of different groups;
5. the special case of forgiveness as defined previously but relating to divine–human relations and also to "three-party" forgiveness – forgiveness from God for offenses against other parties or forgiveness extended by humans to humans in emulation of God; and
6. forgiveness and mercy as intrinsic aspects of the divine character and so a structural aspect of the divine governance of the world.

Forgiveness is a kind of excess, an excess of mercy or deferred retaliation, measured against some standard of what would otherwise be just and appropriate. The aforementioned various meanings can be grouped into three different orders of excess: an excess on the plane of individual relations (and their psychic interiors), an excess operational in the life of groups or communities, and a universal excess characteristic of the divine nature with application to all. We will touch on all of these.

Forgiveness in the theological sense cannot be exhausted in any one of these dimensions, and one aspect is balanced or corrected by others. So, for instance, a religious imperative to "forgive always" might be inferred from viewing forgiveness entirely as a spiritual perfection based on imitation of an intrinsic feature of God's character. But applying that imperative, in a manner that undercuts accountability for and resistance to abuse or oppression, can perpetuate evil precisely by ignoring other dimensions of the good forgiveness intends to realize: the moral and spiritual healing of both victim and perpetrator, the just functioning of the group, and the construction of a better future in the fullness of divine governance.

The study of forgiveness may frequently be limited to one or a few of these dimensions. For instance, there is much contemporary research on forgiveness that addresses it almost exclusively in terms of point 2: what we might call "therapeutic forgiveness" for persons, focused on the subjective well-being occasioned by "letting go" anger and antagonism toward offenders.[2] Similarly, efforts at "restorative justice" attend particularly to forgiveness in terms of point 4, the social benefits that can be achieved by deferring legal punishments in favor of processes that seek reconciliation (Schimmel 2002: 136).

Monotheism

In this discussion, I focus on monotheism as a distinctive form of axial age religion, as described by Robert Bellah (2011). He distinguishes different stages of religion that have corresponded to different stages of human culture: mimetic, mythical, and theoretic. In the mimetic stage, religion takes form in the ritual, music, and rhythm that enable early forms of culture and human solidarity – a unity fostered through heightened and shared experience. In the mythical stage, language enables a narrative understanding of the world that is in tension with the one before us in immediate consciousness. The axial age religions – most of what we think of as "world religions" – arise in theoretic culture (with its second-order conceptions of transcendence and universality) or are themselves determinants of it. Bellah regards these forms of religion as cumulative within any single tradition, not as successive replacements for each other. The "conserved core processes" of mimetic ritual and mythic narrative live on within the theoretic frame of later traditions (Heim 2014).

Axial age religions are characterized by a new sense of transcendence. They stand at a point of transition where oral culture and the storage of individual brains is supplemented with external, written media and where theory construction (thinking about thinking) joins narrative reasoning. This second-order reflection brings both a critical edge toward prior forms (antiritualism and demythologization) and a radical capacity to systematically imagine a world alternative to that of ordinary experience and intuitive reason. Monotheisms framed this dimension of transcendence in terms of a personal, creator God, who could not be defined as a being within the ordinary world. This was not the only path to the axial age breakthrough, as is evident in Buddhism, the contrast case I consider in our first section.

Monotheisms are not homogenous within a single monotheistic tradition or across them all. This is partly because of the conservation of the mimetic and

---

[2] See further discussion of this in Section 1.

mythical dimensions that Bellah mentions: ritual and narrative features in Judaism, Christianity, and Islam retain their distinctive characters and so "flavor" the common affirmation of the one God. And it is partly so because "pure monotheism" is itself a regulative aspiration rather than a settled fact, both at the origin of these traditions and in their current expressions (Assmann 2010: 32–33). In Jan Assman's view, what distinguishes monotheistic traditions is less the affirmation of one god versus many than the affirmation of a true religion versus false religions. Monotheistic transcendence involves an inescapable ethical element, relational *accountability* particularly relevant to our topic of forgiveness. One truth, a common standard and norm, is as central to monotheism as a numerical singularity in God (Assmann 2010: 21). In this respect, the monotheistic origins of the positive universals in a modern classically liberal view of the world (regarding scientific truth, human rights, dignity, and knowledge) are bound up also with much that a postmodern liberal view increasingly contests as a negative side of universal claims: exclusivism, ideological and religious violence, and pseudo-objectivity (Schwartz 1997). This Element does not go into that particular debate over monotheism, but I mention it because this backdrop suggests that the topic of forgiveness has wide cultural significance.

Plan of the Element

This Element aims to sketch the general shape of the question of forgiveness in the context of monotheistic traditions. Since the topic is vast and its possible contact points with other fields legion, I have chosen some illustrative theological engagements. The three sections are intended as distinct but interwoven essays. They offer three kinds of introduction: an introduction by contrast, an introduction through variation, and an introduction by application.

The first section deals with a comparative case to explore what difference it makes to conceive forgiveness on a monotheistic basis. I consider the character of forbearance in Buddhism and the extent to which it covers the same practical ground and behavior as our topic. This gives us some basis to judge how far monotheistic traditions may be constitutive of familiar cultural connotations of forgiveness. Without the belief in one God – a creator and moral arbiter on the one hand and a merciful lover of humanity on the other – it is not clear that forgiveness would be a central metaphysical, religious topic, as well as a practical, ethical one.

The second section looks to the three traditions – Judaism, Christianity, and Islam – that affirm belief in one God and claim common historical descent from the same figure, as "Abrahamic religions." I explore their teachings on forgiveness as a theme with variations. I seek to fill out our understanding of the topic through the description of their common assumptions and their divergent perspectives. The section explores shared elements such as repentance, sin, intercession, and reconciliation and describes some variations in thinking and practice across the faiths. I focus in a few cases on ways in which Christian views are "outliers" in respect to the others. I do this not to intervene in these long-standing intra-Abrahamic arguments but as a strategy for an introductory text. I think such an approach is the most efficient way to illustrate some of the wider issues, as opposed to a bland "three corners" description. I believe the questions touched on in this way are those that most often come up in intra-Abrahamic conversations about forgiveness, whether informal or scholarly, and so may offer the reader a point of contact.

In the third section, I consider one major area where theological views of forgiveness interact with secular and scientific views. The first section already touches briefly on connections with psychology and therapeutic perspectives with particular application to individuals. The third section turns to evolutionary and cognitive study of religion, focusing particularly on social and community life. Recent work in this area offers some very suggestive insights as to how the "excess" of forgiveness explicitly thematized and promoted by monotheistic traditions is woven into human life and development. I lay out a brief constructive argument on this score, one that I hope may stimulate further reflection upon our question.

I am a Christian theologian who has worked in the area of comparative theology, and this Element purposely (and no doubt implicitly) reflects that perspective.

1 Forbearance and Forgiveness

> Some do wrong out of delusion, while others, being deluded, become angry.
> Among them, whom do we call innocent, and whom do we call guilty?
> (Śāntideva, Wallace, and Wallace 1997: 69)

Questions of retaliation and reconciliation are endemic to human life. They arise whether or not the population of actors includes spirits and divinities as well as human agents. Religions historically played a central role in defining what counts as offenses in human behavior and in prescribing the punishments appropriate to these transgressions. In many indigenous traditions, we observe both a strong norm requiring retaliation in kind for violence, particularly killing, and also established practices in which the strict symmetry of violence may be modulated on the basis of economic compensation and ritual interactions among the parties. Religious practices were central in tending the boundary between injury and retaliation: resolving feuds, setting the scope of retribution, and ostracizing or rehabilitating offenders. Religious bodies often still maintain their own venues to adjudicate and remediate spiritual violations to which the wider society is indifferent or to bring to bear their distinctive standards for reconciliation on matters of family or commercial law. Such religious regulation of retaliation and reconciliation virtually always includes some measure of forgiveness as we have defined it in the introduction.

Striking practices and teachings of forgiveness appear within all religious traditions. It would be fruitless to globally characterize some as more forgiving than others, without considering the more specific meanings of such an expectation or obligation in each one. Clearly, the beliefs and behaviors within which forgiveness features constellate differently in different traditions. The result is a corresponding variety of views on the problems forgiveness addresses, the rationale for its practice, and the extent and centrality of its role in religious realization. In this section, we approach the question of forgiveness and monotheism by way of contrast. We consider how much of the substance of forgiveness may be framed on the basis of an alternative tradition, that of Buddhism, and suggest what distinctive features in monotheism emerge by comparison.

1.1 Monotheism

Belief in a single, personal, creator God adds a distinctive agent to the equation of retaliation and reconciliation. In a world with multiple divine powers, it seems that human issues of retaliation or non-retaliation arise on a larger scale but in the same shape. In such a setting, it makes sense to ask how betrayals and violence are resolved among the gods, whether one divine spirit punishes a human's lapse or change in devotion and whether a human adherent might forgive a deity for failure to deliver on promised or implied supernatural benefits.

Monotheism posits a universal relation and so the possibility that forgiveness could have a universal reference. All of us stand in the same or similar status with regard to God. In the three Abrahamic traditions, it is clear that every two-party problem of forgiveness is in fact a three-party problem. No offense against my neighbor, and no resolution of that offense, is a purely private matter, in moral or practical terms. There are transgressions (as from the first table of the Ten Commandments – worshipping false gods and taking God's name in vain) that apply only to my relation with God and for which rectification must be sought directly with God. Divine forgiveness becomes a new and additional need, alongside any others. Other transgressions (as from the second table of the Ten Commandments) in the first instance affect other persons, and their rectification involves those persons as well as God. Indeed, the scope of these transgressions expands to include an interior dimension, a dimension entirely unknown to those against whom the transgression is aimed (coveting someone's goods, resenting their success, and wishing them evil). God observes and registers these things, and God also figures among the injured parties insofar as it is God's commandments that have been violated.

Monotheism concentrates forgiveness in terms of a shared relation. The divine is centered in a single supreme source, and this source is sharply distinguished from the universe as its contingent creation. In this way, monotheism sets the stage for understanding forgiveness as a cosmic issue. Dualisms or polytheisms may attribute merciful and beneficent care for human beings to some powers and moral accountability and punishment to others. A vengeful deity may conflict with an indulgent one. On the other hand, monistic or nondualistic religious perspectives may find no ontic or relational rupture that requires the specific repair that forgiveness seeks. A monotheistic view sees relation with God as every being's business and the administration of both justice and mercy as belonging to the same ultimate agent. The question of forgiveness and reconciliation thus becomes in some measure an internal issue in the divine life and also acquires a common universal character.

1.2 Buddhism and Forbearance

Buddhism is perhaps the most explicit anti-monotheistic of the world's large religions. It generally does not question the existence of "gods" in the sense of beings in the conventional world whose powers and capacities surpass those of humans (Keown 2013: 37). It affirms the existence of events and states (such as reincarnation or omniscient consciousness) that are supernatural by normal accounts. And Buddhism shares with other axial age religions belief in a single, transcendent order or truth, which it calls the *dharma*. But virtually, all forms of Buddhism explicitly reject the idea of a single, transcendent, personal, creator God and so reject monotheism as understood in this Element. For our purposes, this makes Buddhism a particularly fruitful comparison point. The comparison can illuminate (1) how much of what we understand as forgiveness is explicitly taught and practiced in Buddhism with no reference to any monotheistic basis and (2) what features of forgiveness are particularly shaped by monotheistic convictions.

1.2.1 The Perfection of Forbearance

Buddhists do not hesitate to use the term "forgiveness" in contemporary teaching. But the tradition favors other terms to describe similar behavior. For an example, we can look to a classic *Mahāyāna* Buddhist text, *A Guide to the*

Bodhisattva Way of Life (Śāntideva, Wallace, and Wallace 1997). Śāntideva, an eighth-century Indian monk, produced this much-loved summary of the path to enlightenment. This Element outlines that path by means of descriptions of the six traditional key perfections of a bodhisattva or Buddha-in-the-making. Śāntideva devotes a chapter to the perfection called forbearance (or, in other translations, patience). It is the perfection whose practice most closely coincides with forgiveness. To cultivate it, we should not retaliate against those that injure us. We should return good for evil. We should abjure any inner ill will toward the offenders.

Indeed, it is this latter dimension that is the hallmark of forbearance. This perfection is paired as the antidote to the specific negative emotion of anger. Anger, in Śāntideva's view, is mainly destructive to the one who experiences it and is to be overcome in all cases by going to the roots where it is generated, to the negative emotions toward others that impel us toward retribution. In this sense, "there is no evil equal to hatred, and no spiritual practice equal to forbearance" (Śāntideva, Crosby, and Skilton 1996: 50). Anger is most resistant where it seems most justified, where revenge and retribution are warranted according to our ordinary sense of justice. We see others as the source of our problems and the destruction or restraint of our offenders as the solution. Forbearance requires that we overcome this as a fundamental misperception.

1.2.2 Three Insights

This requires three insights. First, we must dispel the association of the suffering we experience with those we take to be its agents. We take the offender as the source of our pain, and our anger at them distracts us from recognizing and attacking its real sources, in our own negative emotions and their causes. Śāntideva says it is just as misguided to be angry with a person who attacks me as it is to be angry at the knife they use. The knife and my body are equally causes of suffering. "He has obtained a weapon, and I have obtained a body. With what should I be angry?" (Śāntideva, Wallace, and Wallace 1997: 66).

Second, in accordance with the basic Buddhist teaching of "no self," there is no one "there" to be angry at, no substantive decision-taking agent who has intended to harm me. The individual selves readily referred to in Buddhist teaching are viewed as useful at the level of conventional reference but lacking any intrinsic substance for an enlightened understanding. Both the actions that offend me and the anger I feel about them arise from antecedent conditions, with no enduring one to be the initiator before or the guilty subject after. We feel no anger toward bile in our bodies that may cause intense pain, so why should we be angry with others whose actions are just as much a confluence of conditioned causes? (Śāntideva, Wallace, and Wallace 1997: 64).

Third, Buddhist teaching allows us to see that the wrongs others do to us "are the direct result of our past actions" (Gyatso 2009: 64). The karmic order has infallibly allocated these results as the consequence of our own prior behavior but presents them also as a priceless opportunity to generate great merit through forbearance and non-retaliation. In this last perspective, the enemy is actually doing us a favor by committing acts that will earn them future karmic punishment while affording us the occasion to improve our karma.

In short, when Buddhists speak in conventional terms of the interaction of selves, they view that interaction more as the result of the causal histories of each self than as a de novo decision of one in regard to the other. When they speak in the terms of "higher" wisdom, selves are no longer a primary reference point at all. Forbearance, as a theory and practice of non-retaliation, could hardly be more radical in scope and depth. It applies to all offenses, of any type, against any person. Vengeance belongs not to us or to the (nonexistent) God but, in a sense, to karma. The causal fruits of evil actions end in hells of suffering, as the causal fruits of selfless actions lead to liberation. Forbearance does not alter that calculus but moves the practitioner to the right side of it. The great bodhisattvas are known for the extremity of their actions on this score. One of the most famous stories of Kuan Yin relates that, although her father had earlier tried to execute her, when he became ill she gouged out both eyes and cut off both arms to make the magic elixir that would heal him (Palmer, Ramsay, and Kwok 2009: 94–97).

Such a radical act of what we might call "forgiveness" follows from dispelling major assumptions present in monotheism, assumptions that create the need and possibility for forgiveness, including all references to God. Buddhist wisdom questions each of the elements that present the problem as monotheism understands it: the enduring existence of the offender who commits the offense, the substantial existence of the one who suffers it, the act as the true cause of the suffering, and even the vector that tells us who is a victim and who is a benefactor.

The fullest benefit for the "victim" comes not only through behavioral non-retaliation, and spiritual understanding of the irrelevance of the supposed harm, but also through the additional wish for the good of the offender, their release from suffering. Among other things, this Buddhist analysis throws into doubt the ability to isolate any specific set of single-agent acts, producing specific person-limited sufferings, out of the ocean of suffering per se. Forbearance is a type of non-retaliation that differs from monotheistic ones in that it does not envision the solidity or continuance of the two (or more) participants in relation who might be a party to the forgiveness. Guilt, shame, and estrangement from others are seen as subsets of universal suffering, floating on the same fundamental ignorance.

We see from Śāntideva's example that both this course of action (returning no evil for evil and refusing to insist on one's own "due") and a profound path to inner emotional and mental peace can be manifest without need for the God of monotheism.

Forbearance is based upon the assertion that the perceived need for forgiveness, like the impulse toward vengeance or anger, is a negative emotion born of misperception. These things appear to be responses to real agents and actions and their challenges to our well-being when, in fact, it is these impulses and emotions that are themselves the challenges we must overcome to be freed.

1.3 Two Parables

As it happens, we have an interesting comparison of these themes in a Buddhist parable (found in the *Lotus Sutra*) and a Christian parable (found in the *Gospel of Luke*).[3] Both of them deal with a father and a lost son, and their parallel structure makes their divergence all the more interesting (Valea 2009: 171 ff).

The biblical parable concerns a father with two sons. The younger one demands to receive his inheritance and departs to live in another city. Falling into poverty, hunger, and desperation, he determines to return home, to confess the hurt he brought to his father, and to humbly request a place as a menial worker in his father's household. The father, seeing him at a distance, runs to meet him and restores him immediately to his family status, throwing a banquet to celebrate this reconciliation. The older son, coming upon this celebration, is outraged and reproaches the father for never having celebrated him in the same manner. The father assures him that he is loved no less.

In its broad lines, the plot of the story in the *Lotus Sutra* is similar. The story concerns a father whose young son runs away to live in a distant city. There he falls into destitution and wanders from place to place in search of survival. The father, who was previously a humble man, becomes rich and powerful but longs for someone to whom he could pass on his possessions and place. By chance, the son happens to be in the place where his father lives. Overawed by this rich man (whom he does not recognize) and actually afraid of his power, the son intends to move on. But the father recognizes him and sends messengers to retrieve him. The son, misunderstanding their intentions, believes he is being enslaved and fights against them. Seeing

---

[3] See Reeves 2008 for the Buddhist parable that is found in chapter 4, "Faith and Understanding." The Christian parable is found in *Luke* 15:11–32.

this, the father takes another tack. He tells the messengers to release the son and then has others approach him to offer the most menial of jobs, clearing dung from stables.

The son accepts, and over many following years, the father superintends the son's steady advancement in responsibilities (sometimes coming incognito in rags to work alongside the son to chastise or encourage him) until a point comes where the son has become worthy to serve as a steward of the entire household, and the father is near death. At that time, the father holds a banquet, announces the lost son's identity, and bestows his inheritance.

The virtues of the *Lotus Sutra* father are very resonant with the understanding of forbearance we discussed previously. The son ran away and abandoned the father (at a time when the father was neither wealthy nor powerful). When the son is discovered and responds to his father's messengers with misplaced anger and fear, the father does not take offense or waver in his intent. He accepts that the distance in status and understanding cannot be immediately bridged. He works patiently and incrementally to improve the child's virtue and knowledge until the transition to the new role is possible. In the end, when the son learns the whole story, he reflects, "Without any intention or effort on my part these treasures have now come to me by themselves" (Reeves 2008: 145).

The root problem for the Buddhist parable is ignorance, in many forms. The son runs away from home because he is "immature and ignorant" (Reeves 2008: 147). When the two do meet, the son does not recognize the father or understand his intentions. Nor does he understand what is truly happening in all the years of apprenticeship and training. Through that time, the relationship between them is conducted through intermediaries and under different guises, as when the father pretends to be a fellow worker or a manager. The wealth of the father represents the liberating wisdom of the *dharma*. The father in the story is clearly the Buddha, and the parable illustrates the skillful means by which truth can be adapted to the stage and condition of the hearer to help them advance.[4] Insofar as the child's ignorance leads him to behave hurtfully toward the father or to require great effort, the father never takes this behavior personally. The focus is less on the restoration of a relationship than on clearing the mind.

The biblical parable shares with the sutra parable only one key element of ignorance, the circumstantial plot device that provides the father does not know where the son has gone. The sutra father contrives a menial job for the son

---

[4] In this sense, it is similar to the more famous parable from the *Lotus Sutra,* the parable of the burning house, in which in order to entice his children to safely flee a burning house, a father promises them toys and sweets.

because it is all the son can comprehend. The biblical son humbles himself with the admission that such a job is better than he deserves. The moment of mutual recognition comes at the very end of the *Lotus Sutra* parable, the culmination. In Jesus's story, there is never any doubt about identities. The son knows where to find home and decides to turn in that direction, with all the messy history that will require him to face. The moment of mutual recognition and acceptance is at the center of the story, prior to any transformation in the child's behavior except an acknowledged need.

The Lukan parable turns around the moment when the father sees the son in the distance and runs to embrace and accept him. In an instant, the father bypasses any punishment or condition for restoration. The celebration that ensues is based on the father's binary exclamation: "For this my son was dead, and is alive again; he was lost, and is found." (Luke 15:24) Forgiveness is an event, experienced interactively. The rest of the parable addresses the fallout from the unexpected excess in the father's proactive embrace of the lost child, including disruption of the relationship of the father with the older child and resesentment of the older child toward the younger one.

Both stories affirm profound care for the lost child. That care is tinged with a stronger tone of wisdom in the one case and a stronger tone of love in the other. The care in the Buddhist story is suffused with understanding, such that it is finally hard to say what, if anything, actually requires forgiveness. The care in the biblical story is suffused with affection that enacts reconciliation before the problem is solved and intimates a future in need of resolution anew.

1.4 Forgiveness as Therapeutic Wisdom

Forbearance, as we have seen it in Śāntideva, focuses *within*. The challenges it addresses arise in our misperceptions and secondarily in the negative emotions that follow from them.

Those emotions project into our construal of events in the world and our corresponding actions. Monotheistic perspectives tend to situate the question of forgiveness *among*. The challenges it addresses arise through our relations with each other and subsequently through the ways these shape our inner subjectivity and our social frameworks. Clearly, the behaviors described by forbearance and forgiveness overlap. But the two do not have the same profile. Experimental approaches to Buddhist religious practice have tended to center on meditation and its effects on measures of health or function, and those to Christian religious practice have turned particularly to forgiveness and its effect not only on inner but also on relational health. In either case, such analysis stresses what we might call a therapeutic dimension, one that centers primarily on an individual (the meditator or the forgiver) and on the practice in terms of tangible benefits in the immediate context.

Much recent scholarly attention to forgiveness takes this form, as an investigation of its effects on mental and physical health (Toussaint et al. 2015). Though clearly taking its lead from forgiveness as understood in the monotheistic traditions, and Christianity in particular, such research defines forgiveness in terms of a victim reducing negative thoughts, emotions, intentions, and behaviors toward the offender and replacing these with positive alternatives.[5] This includes both "decisional" and "emotional" aspects, sometimes distinguished to the point of being two different types of forgiveness (Tucker et al. 2015). Decisional forgiveness is largely behavioral, cognitive, and outward-facing. It adopts a posture of non-retaliation, in consonance with religious or social norms and in the interests of maintaining specific relationships or a web of relations. Emotional forgiveness involves some kind of empathetic revision of the felt attitude toward an offender and a transformation or healing of one's own negative emotions.

The location of much of this research in psychology departments and in public health or medical schools means that the effects of forgiveness are measured in parameters that range from blood pressure and cardiovascular risk levels to mental health variables. The operative hypothesis is that forgiveness is beneficial to the well-being of the one who practices it (and, less often studied, for the person forgiven). The overarching framework for most of this work is a "stress-and-coping" theory that sees forgiveness improving mental and physical health by mitigating the stress that arises from experienced injury or offense (Toussaint et al. 2015). In experimental terms, forgiveness is measured by scores on inventories or scales regarding a subject's attitudes toward self-forgiveness, other forgiveness, and divine forgiveness. Such scales ask respondents to express their level of agreement with statements like "I have forgiven those who hurt me," "I have forgiven myself for things I have done wrong," "Although this person's action hurt me, I have goodwill toward that person," and "I know that God or a higher power forgives me."

An example of this literature would be a recent longitudinal study of young adults that found all of the forgiveness measures utilized "were positively associated with psychosocial well-being outcomes, and inversely associated with depressive and anxiety symptoms" (Chen et al. 2019). Controlling for multiple variables, the association of forgiveness with lowered rates of mental illness and health-related conditions (obesity, smoking, and eating disorders) has even led

---

[5] This definition is paraphrased from VanderWeele 2018.

some to commend its consideration as a public health issue (VanderWeele 2018). Along these same lines, psychologists and counselors have developed interventions and workbooks aimed at enhancing people's practice of forgiveness.[6] These therapeutic approaches deal with important aspects of forgiveness and bring the discussion into a common arena where it can be acknowledged and encouraged from secular and varied religious perspectives. The benefit of this clarity and focus comes with a coordinate limitation, as its framework does not begin to approximate a full theological perspective.

Forgiveness figures here as a form of enlightened self-interest. As stated in one of the "nine steps" in forgiveness articulated in the Stanford Forgiveness Project, "Make a commitment to yourself to do what you have to do to feel better. Forgiveness is for you and not for anyone else" (Luskin 2020). Whatever harm may have been done in the precipitating offense, a non-forgiving disposition only exacerbates and intensifies it. The mercy that the practice extends is directed first and most certainly to the one who practices it.

This is by no means to suggest that such approaches are indifferent to the social application of forgiveness. The interventions developed are in many cases explicitly applied to persons in the context of searing conflicts like those in Northern Ireland, in Israel/Palestine, or in the aftermath of the Rwandan genocide.[7] In such settings, the therapeutic healing of individuals is seen as a precondition and precursor of wider social restoration. In Section 3, we will explore a research avenue that is distinct from but complementary to this orientation, looking at forgiveness more from a social than a psychological perspective.

1.5 Monotheism and the Future

Our brief consideration of forbearance demonstrates that Buddhism offers an explicitly non-monotheistic practice and theory of much that is included in forgiveness. Buddhist analysis deconstructs the basis for the problem forgiveness ostensibly solves, the problem of guilt and restoration of relation. Forbearance is commended by reference to the impermanent or illusory character of the perceived realities that constitute such problems. Underlying assumptions that fuel notions of revenge, punishment, bitterness, or even of justice are deconstructed. When these things are seen as they actually are, the impetus toward retaliation, blame, or guilt dissipates, and "forgiveness" – in the sense of non-retaliation and passing over others' offenses – is the outcome that follows.

---

[6] See a review and evaluation in Wade, Worthington, and Meyer 2005.
[7] For example, see Bettencourt 2015.

It is not just that there is no superperson, God, with whom we might need reconciliation. There are not actually any others, or even an enduring "I," to be in conflict, to constitute injured or offending parties. The connotations of "forbearance" in contrast to "forgiveness" are relevant here. Forgiveness typically suggests an affirmative act responsive to other persons. It has a directional, relational orientation. Forbearance suggests more that one refrains from composing the constituent emotions and delusions that lead to the suffering associated with injury, guilt, and resentment. This nonpersonal analysis can be a benefit, avoiding the sometimes toxic residue that can subsist in relations between forgivers and forgiven who understand themselves in those terms.

These comparisons highlight certain common elements in monotheism that contrast with Buddhist approaches. The first is the respect in which monotheism understands forgiveness on a permanent relational basis. It is not just that the personal creator God adds another agent to the population of all those who might be a party to forgiveness. By instituting the fundamental distinction of creator and creation, monotheism also recognizes one irreducible relation, one case in which the very assumptions that Buddhism rejects are taken as fundamental. This relation becomes the guarantor of innumerable others, the relations among creatures, including persons. Viewed in this way, forgiveness is first a universal question, framed between God and creatures, and then derivatively a distributed, interpersonal one.

The monotheistic and Buddhist behavioral injunctions on forgiveness/forbearance largely overlap, but the basis for them is distinctly different. Impermanence is key to Buddhist forbearance. We can let go of others' injuries to us or the effect of our actions on them because nothing has the kind of weight that would justify holding on to them. Forbearance is implied by the fleetingness of all. In monotheism, forgiveness is impelled by the preservation of what is healed. A monotheistic understanding of creatureliness has a certain empirical agreement with Buddhism. If impermanence means to lack control of one's own existence, to be intrinsically dependent, then monotheists agree that all creation (though not the God who made it) is impermanent. But if to be impermanent necessarily means to be destined to disappear entirely as a participant in relation or as a distinguishable subject, then they do not believe all creation is impermanent. For monotheists, forgiveness makes an enduring difference for persons and their relations, both of which are themselves of enduring significance.[8]

Forgiveness is of crucial importance for those who anticipate a future together. We can see this in concrete terms, in that forgiveness can be

---

[8] For a fuller discussion of the topics in this paragraph, see Heim 2019.

a consuming concern within families, or marriages, or tight-knit groups – settings where people either have no choice about whether to continue to live in close connection or else deeply desire to continue to do so. People may perceive that forgiveness and reconciliation are, literally, the only way that they will be able to have a livable future. When unresolved transgressions afflict relations from which there is no escape or for which we cannot relinquish hope, it is as though we must walk continually on a wounded or broken leg. The tension over unreconciled injuries and betrayals is a constant source of new pain, an unavoidable drain of energy, and a barrier to new beginnings.

Eschatology, the expectation among monotheistic faiths for a final consummation and a future life of God with creatures, expresses this future dimension in a universal way.

Repentance, forgiveness, and reconciliation are necessities because there is a continuing story for the divine with humans, and for persons with each other, beyond what we may empirically see. In this sense, Jurgen Moltmann says, all forms of repentance and forgiveness are a kind of conversion, "an 'about turn.' And this turn is a turn to the future . . . to the future of the living God" (Moltmann and Moltmann 1980: 24). Forgiveness is not simply about resolving the past or healing the present. It is preparation for the future, one in which both the persons and the relations that have been wounded will take part.

2 Forgiveness within and among the Abrahamic Monotheisms

> God does not deal with us according to our sins,
> Nor repay us according to our iniquities.
> For as the heavens are high above the earth,
> > So great is his steadfast love toward those who fear him;
> As far as the east is from the west,
> > So far he removes our transgressions from us.
> > > –Psalm 103:10–12[9]

In the last section, we saw that the theory and practice of non-retaliation are alive and well in a non-monotheistic tradition, Buddhism. We also indicated that monotheism constitutes its understanding of forgiveness on a different basis and so effectively diverges in understanding its character and reach. In this section, we will describe common features of forgiveness in monotheism and trace some of its variations in Judaism, Christianity, and Islam.

---

[9] Unless otherwise noted, this and all subsequent biblical quotations are from the New Revised Standard Version.

2.1 A God Who Forgives

The Abrahamic God is a forgiving God. Exodus 34:6–7, scripture for both Jews and Christians, says, "The Lord, the Lord, a God merciful and gracious, slow to anger, and abounding in steadfast love and faithfulness, keeping steadfast love for the thousandth generation, forgiving iniquity and transgression and sin . . . ." Jesus's disciples asked not whether to forgive but how often, and he told them they should do so seven times seventy times (Matthew 18:21–22).

The most common form for the celebration of the Eucharist, when bread and wine are received, says of the cup that it is the blood of Christ, "poured out for the forgiveness of sins" (Matthew 26:28). The Qur'an, in Surah 6:54, says "Surely God is the most forgiving and the most merciful." No term for God is more ubiquitous in Islam than *Al-Rahman Al-Rahim*, "the most gracious, the most merciful." This form of address is repeated in each of the five daily prayers and stands at the beginning of every Surah in the Qur'an save one. It is a kind of pulse in Muslim devotion. The same root word in Hebrew, derived from that for womb, appears with similar regularity in Jewish scripture and devotion, referring to God's mercy and steadfast love: "I desire mercy and not sacrifice" (Hosea 6:6). The prophet Micah asks "Who is God like You, who pardons sin and forgives the transgression of the remnant of his inheritance? You do not stay angry forever but delight to show mercy" (Micah 7:18, NIV). For Israel and subsequently for Rabbinic Judaism, Christianity, and Islam, this quality is one of the identifying characteristics of the God who is to be worshiped, helping pick that God out from among other supposed deities or from false characterizations.

Belief in God's forgiveness is not only asserted as a theoretical moral ideal. It is acted out in the narrative of God's dealings with the people of Israel, who fall out of covenant faithfulness and are repeatedly called and accepted back into that covenant despite disobedience. This divine attribute is reflected in human paragons within each tradition. It is a central element in the story of Joseph. It is reflected in Jesus's response to his own enemies and in central events in the life of disciples like Paul or Stephen. It is manifest in the behavior of Mohammad, particularly in the gracious treatment of his defeated Meccan adversaries. Forgiveness figures as a spiritual ideal in all three traditions, necessary for reestablishing and maintaining human community with God. Ritual or devotional provisions for responding to sin revolve around appeals to and trust in divine forbearance and mercy.

Yet this is not the whole story. The Exodus passage quoted previously affirms that God forgives iniquity, transgression, and sin. But it immediately continues, "yet by no means clearing the guilty, but visiting the iniquity of the parents upon the children and the children's children, to the third and the fourth generation" (Exodus 34:7). Mercy is, first of all, a holding off from punitive action. This is different from the Buddhist perfection of forbearance, which dispels the assumptions upon which retribution rests. This mercy is the deferral of entirely justified wrath on God's part, against actions and harms that are all too real. God defers retribution, to give time for repentance and reform. This interim forgiveness can be made permanent by a change of course on the part of the offender. If not, then the Exodus text suggests that the consequences of transgression will still be applied to later generations who are found persisting in the same sin. Clearly, here, we have to do with a strong corporate and communal sense of responsibility. This dimension of meaning is supplemented but not entirely displaced, in all the Abrahamic faiths, when the question of forgiveness is applied primarily to individuals. In that application, the deferral is referred not to future generations but to a final judgment that awaits persons.

2.2 Monotheistic Concentration

The recognition of a single, personal creator concentrates the issue of forgiveness in two important ways. On the one hand, it focuses the question within the nature of God, where there is an unavoidable tension between justice and mercy. On the other hand, it defines the question as a dynamic between the creator and all human creatures, pressing toward an account of forgiveness as a universal issue, not only a circumstantial, local, or private one.

2.2.1 Within God

The first concentration unifies the administration of justice and mercy in one set of hands. Dualisms or polytheisms may encompass gods of judgment and gods of mercy, a cruel, indifferent god, and a benevolent god. In the monotheistic world, God must manage both ultimate adjudication and ultimate remediation. God is the final guarantor of the moral world, the norm against which wrongness is measured and the supreme source of mercy. This tension dwells in the character of God. Just as forgiveness has to do not only with a course of action but also with the inner life of forgiver and forgiven, so too the monotheistic concentration means that theology must address not only the divine course of action but also the inner life or consistency of the divine actor.

The theodicy question, a shared challenge for the Abrahamic traditions, expresses this tension. The challenge exists because monotheists hold so firmly to the premises just mentioned. God's character, in first allowing and then passing over evil and its attendant suffering without immediate remedy or revenge, is put on trial. How can God be both good and all-powerful when justice is not done in history? God's practice of forgiveness and mercy may only aggravate this question, multiplying the instances in which God fails to be just by our reckoning. Forgiveness, which figures in monotheistic traditions as a key to the prospective solution of human sinfulness, at the same time appears to heighten the challenge as to how God's consummation of history can keep faith with both righteousness and mercy.

The intensity of the question encourages a practical, implicit pull toward a partial dualism. God's choice for a world with human freedom and emergent corrupting forces allows subordinate agents to become responsible for instigating disorder and pain in the world. Satan and human free will become sources of evil. Yet God is still responsible for balancing justice and mercy in the response to that evil. In popular culture, Satan is usually represented at one of two extremes. He is seen as a prince of leniency, who advocates a regime in which everything is permitted. Or he is viewed as the paragon of inflexible justice, who insists on the letter of the law against all forms of mercy. Libertine or legalist, Satan appears to forgive everything or to forgive nothing and to be able to lead humans astray on either premise. These two poles represent the temptations to which God is presumed not to succumb. In one, forgiveness loses all claim to righteousness, and in the other, justice itself becomes oppressive cruelty.

This tension is reflected in the stories of Job and Jonah, stories shared by the three traditions.[10] In the case of Job, the Satan who instigates Job's ordeal is an in-house prosecutor, who rejects out of hand any laxity in the application of the law and who insists on testing Job's purity by a trial of gratuitous suffering. Job must be perfectly righteous or forfeit God's favor – an opinion God at least initially shares. Jonah's story is that of a reluctant prophet, who initially flees the call to preach repentance to his hated enemies, the Ninevites, and then is bitterly disappointed to see their change of heart met with God's ready pardon. The story of Job raises the question of the unjust suffering of the righteous or innocent. The story of Jonah raises what in some ways is a complementary concern. Jonah protests against the divine forgiveness of the wicked.[11] The buck stops with God on both fronts.

---

[10] This paragraph refers to the text of these stories in the Hebrew scriptures shared by Christians. In the Qur'an, the Job story is dramatically condensed and the Jonah story diverges somewhat from the biblical version. Though the biblical text gives more space to a "protest" dimension in Jonah and Job's relations with God, all three traditions often muted this element in practice: Jews by stressing God's inscrutability, Christians by overlaying a typological and Christological reading, and Muslims by stressing the conformity of both figures to the ideal role of prophets. For the Qur'anic version, see Nasr et al. 2015.

[11] The book of Jonah is read as a central text at Yom Kippur (Day of Atonement). In that context, it stands as a hopeful assurance that with repentance, divine forgiveness is possible.

2.2.2 Between God and Creation

The second monotheistic concentration stems from the distinction made between the creator and the creation, a distinction that is moral as well as metaphysical. All creatures and all persons have an equally intimate, immediate relation with God. This is the single universal relation, applying to all and constitutive of the well-being of each. If that relation becomes broken for all people, forgiveness is no longer an episodic option, whose relevance and realization come and go in the interactions among various human agents. Nor can it be treated primarily as a "subjective" issue about overcoming negative emotions, particularly anger, and their effects, as with Buddhist forbearance. In connection with God, it becomes a fundamental relational issue for all.

Monotheism introduces a universal standard for moral and spiritual transgression, and for what does or does not stand in need of forgiveness. Forgiveness is different, depending upon the notion of justice it is coordinated with, which defines what counts as requiring forgiveness. Ethical monotheism provides, in principle, a new specification of forgiveness by giving a consistent, universal standard for transgression. By this standard, insofar as all human beings are understood to have violated it, forgiveness is a universal need, whose resolution is necessary for the fulfillment of the divine purpose in creation.

If the need for forgiveness exists in relation to God, it is of supreme importance. This need encompasses healing for negative emotions (self-hatred, envy, and self-righteousness) that primarily harm the one who experiences them, since our own well-being is God's desire and aim. In twisting ourselves into destructive modalities or undervaluing ourselves, we harm God's creation. But, of course, the need for mercy likewise encompasses behaviors that are objectively harmful to others, without explicit reference to God, as well as activities offending God that have no apparent effect on others. The Abrahamic traditions agree that transgression and estrangement in all of these registers apply to all of humanity and that divine forgiveness is a necessary component of the needed healing. This introduces a profound collective dimension to the question. Though the specifics of the offenses may vary from person to person, there is deep solidarity and commonality in the reality of this condition for all people. There are variations among (and to some extent within) the monotheistic traditions, as we shall see, as to the shared structural nature of that estrangement and so as to the characterization of forgiveness.

Both aspects of "monotheistic concentration" come together in the common eschatological spirit of the Abrahamic traditions. We mentioned in the last section that forgiveness is crucial for parties who have a future together. The eschatological expectation of a final judgment and consummation constitutes the horizon of that common future. In this sense, forgiveness is not only an instrumental action necessary on the path to religious realization but also a distinctive feature of that realization. To have become reconciled (pardoned and pardoning) out of our injuries and transgressions and to have ceased to generate new needs for mercy are the substance of salvation or redemption itself.

We see, then, that monotheism's common convictions frame the meaning of forgiveness in a distinctive way and raise some common problems. These include the problem of how to balance the understanding of forgiveness (provisional or unconditional) with justice (final judgment and order) within God and the problem of how to characterize and resolve the universal need for forgiveness of humans in relation to God.

2.3 Common Elements

2.3.1 A Common Story

There is a narrative common to the three traditions in which forgiveness is a key element: the story of Joseph. The two accounts (in Genesis and the Qur'an) are largely consistent. They describe how Joseph, the favored younger among Jacob's twelve sons, was sold into slavery by his jealous siblings. He rose to a position of power in Egypt, prophetically foresaw a famine and organized preparation for it, and so was able finally to offer sustenance to those same brothers when they came seeking help in their desperate hunger. Though all three traditions find varied themes for reflection in this rich story, Jewish, Christian, and Muslim commentators agree that Joseph's forgiveness of the brothers who sold him into slavery is a cardinal feature of the text.[12] That behavior is both a figurative indication of God's attitude and a model for the behavior of believers.

In monotheism, forgiveness is part of the story of humanity with God. In dealing with any case of retribution or forbearance, one must consider not only how this interaction has affected two human parties but also how it relates to God and how it may figure in wider providential processes. In weaving the Joseph story firmly into their own distinctive frameworks, each tradition reflects this shared approach to forgiveness. Jewish commentary stresses several features. One of those is the family dynamic. Joseph, his brothers, and his parents are a people, the ancestors of all Israel. There is more to the picture than balancing the books between Joseph and those individuals who

---

[12] See part 3 in Gregg 2015.

sold him into slavery. There is the question of reconciling and renewing the community, which will be the vehicle of God's future plans. In this respect, Joseph's forbearance is understood looking forward, his life in Egypt fore-shadowing the descent of the people of Israel into Egypt and the rise of Moses, who also would become a prince in that land. Christian commentary likewise stresses a typological view. The brothers' casting of Joseph into a well is likened to the death of Jesus, and Joseph's role in redeeming Egypt and surrounding lands from famine is understood in terms of the spread of the gospel to the whole world. Islamic tradition regards Joseph as a prophet, the role of which Mohammad represents the perfection. The Qur'an calls the story of Joseph "the most beautiful of stories." Muslim commentators say this is so because Joseph models in such breadth both the spiritual and the worldly life of a faithful believer (Nasr et al. 2015: 591). Forgiveness is thus never entirely a purely personal matter. It can relate both to a specific prophetic or messianic calling and point to God's characteristic role in the entire plotline of redemption.

When Joseph reveals his true identity to his brothers, he forestalls their fear of punishment by saying "Now, do not be distressed or reproach yourselves because you sold me hither; it was to save life that God sent me ahead of you. It was not you who sent me here, but God" (Gen 45:5–8)." Joseph can forgive in the knowledge that there is a "rightness" in the actions against him, in a larger providential scheme of God. God can use the offending acts to an effect different from that intended by the actors, and the offenders can sometimes be forgiven in the conviction that they were secondary instruments in a greater plan. By sending him into slavery in Egypt, Joseph's brothers made it possible for him to save multitudes from famine. Joseph's story is unusual in that we are given a bird's-eye view that sets the interpersonal offense against the backdrop of this bigger picture.

Later in the story, when the brothers again fear retaliation from him, Joseph reiterates his forgiveness but in a somewhat different mode, "Have no fear! Am I a substitute for God? Besides, although you intended me harm, God intended it for good" (Gen. 50:19–20). On this occasion, Joseph quite explicitly holds the brothers responsible for the malevolent nature of their acts. They wished him harm and had no aim to serve God's purposes. Though they might have played their role in a greater purpose, this does not truly absolve them. Joseph's forgiveness is couched in terms of the deferral of punishment we mentioned earlier. He will not act as a substitute for God (to whom vengeance ultimately belongs). His forgiveness is an act of humility, a refusal to act in God's place. Judgement for his brothers may be remanded to the proper authority, not necessarily dismissed entirely.

In this case, human mercy has a "governance" dimension, a readiness to refer the matter with confidence to a higher court. From that perspective, it is not a way for humans to liken themselves to God but a way of distinguishing themselves from God. We have neither God's wisdom nor power. It is for God alone to judge. There is another consideration that points in the same direction. We should not presume to judge, not only because we cannot pretend to have a divine perspective but also because we are keenly aware of our own temptations and evils. The most common Christian prayer includes the request "Forgive us our debts, as we also have forgiven our debtors."[13] The act of forgiveness is at the same time an act of intercession seeking to receive the same mercy.

The practice of mercy is related to governance also in that it rests on respect for the original goodness of creation and of persons as they came from God's hand. Evil is a corruption of what remains sound in its original nature. One Muslim scholar suggests that Joseph could view his brother's behavior as coming from the instigation of Satan and not their own initiative. "Joseph takes us to a spiritual vantage point from which it is easy to liberate ourselves from the desire for revenge against those who may have wronged us. For he sees, on the one hand, the intrinsic purity of the soul's nature, the *fitrah,* and, on the other, the extrinsic source of its corruption" (Shah-Kazemi 2019: 44).

The exercise of forgiveness, even in its mundane interpersonal forms, takes on a religious quality. We just noted that in relation to punishment or vengeance, this can take the form of conscious refusal to act in God's place. But forgiveness can also be framed as a positive imitation of God, since God is taken to be preeminently merciful. Jesus teaches "Be merciful, just as your Father is merciful" (Luke 36). Commentators in the Abrahamic traditions all stress that Joseph acted in conformity with his knowledge of God's essential nature. God is merciful *and* just. One practices forgiveness not only in imitation and witness of the divine mercy but also in trust that there is a divine judgment and justice. Not only what punishment will eventually be levied against offenders but also whether in any particular case any punishment at all will be required is left to God. In Islamic tradition, it is said that when Mohammad entered the city of Mecca and his former opponents were helpless before him, he told them "As Joseph said to his brothers, there is no reproach against you. Go, for you are free" (Nasr et al. 2015: 611).

To act in the manner of Joseph is humanly "excessive." It is an affirmative, aspirational imitation of God's nature, a humble recognition that we are not fit to assume God's place, an implicit plea for God's mercy toward us, and an

---

[13] The Lord's Prayer. See Matthew 6:9–13 and Luke 11:2–4.

honoring of the divine image and intent lodged in every person. It gives up what are taken to be normal human prerogatives (retribution and justice), as a testimony to God and God's character. For all three traditions, Joseph represents these same core features.

2.3.2 Repentance and Forgiveness

In monotheistic traditions, forgiveness always goes hand in hand with repentance as its normal condition or accompaniment. The default pattern involves a deferral and perhaps dismissal of judgment in response to a request. It is a merciful act, a departure from strict justice, to accept repentance in lieu of direct, proportional retribution. The prophets of Israel bring just such good news as the flip side of their condemnation of the people's iniquities: God will accept repentance and forgo extracting strict justice. God is being gracious by extending the time to become repentant, in addition to the prior grace of accepting repentance in place of any actual punishment.

In Islam, prophets have been sent to all peoples as "warners" to invite humanity to the right path of worship of the one God. As the ultimate "warner," Mohammad brings this same message. The prophets of Israel couch their message as a call to return, to turn around. The ministry of Jesus actually begins with that of John the Baptist, whose preaching is entirely centered on this one theme of repentance. Repentance seems to be coded into the meaning of "forgiveness" itself. To say that God is merciful is to say that in the face of repentance, God foregoes retaliation and provides restoration, beyond anything that the acts of repentance could be said to deserve on their own.

Forgiveness is an option that belongs to the injured, while repentance is one that belongs to the offender. It is a conversion from wrongdoing. Repentance requires a sincere acknowledgment of what has been done and sincere sorrow over it, coupled with a tangible effort toward restitution. It is a regret whose authenticity is signaled by some costly act or behavior. This may include "making good" the effect of specific offenses (returning more than was stolen, for instance) for those harmed. In addition to this, or in substitution (when direct confession and restoration to the victim is not possible), there are forms of self-denial such as fasting or the "sackcloth and ashes" of public humility and acts of general benevolence toward those in need, who are stand-ins of a sort for the injured party. Neither outward acts (however, impressive) without an inner spirit of reform nor inner attitudes (however, fervent) without tangible expression constitute true repentance.

An offense against another person should be followed by the two-party activities of confession/apology and restitution. This should also be combined with confession and repentance before God. Those offenses that have God alone as their primary object must be addressed in relation to God, but this typically involves some "third party" as well. Just as self-denial and confession explicitly shaped by the religious community may be features of the person-to-person restitution for offenses we commit against each other, so ritual practices and good acts toward other persons may be complementary manifestations of the authenticity of our spiritual repentance for acts against God. Forgiveness accepts less than is expected in terms of retribution or justice. Repentance signals its validity by offering "more" than is normal in some representative way, whether more than exact one-to-one restitution of lost goods to the victim, or more than normal religious observance (exceptional fasting) or an unusual standard of conduct (gratuitous acts of benefit for others). Repentance extends in the direction of God and neighbor and is lacking if it does not find expression in both dimensions.

The Abrahamic traditions express these dimensions in practice and ritual: in forms of self-examination to identify the offenses in need of repentance, in forms of confession and restitution to manifest that repentance, and in forms of reconciliation or absolution to represent forgiveness received. All of these traditions affirm a prophetic strand in their teaching, one that challenges adherents to recognize blindness toward their own need for repentance and forgiveness. In Judaism, no instance looms larger than Yom Kipper, the Day of Atonement, with its sober self-testing, its communal confession, and its liturgical recollection of God's justice and mercy. In Christianity, the Lenten season has a somewhat similar character, a collective intensification of what in both the Eastern and the Western church was historically a year-round individual sacramental practice of confession of sins, acts of penance, and ritual absolution (assurance of forgiveness). In Islam, the five daily prayers are constant occasions for self-assessment, and the personal prayers each individual is encouraged to add to the shared ritual will often revolve around forgiveness. Certain times are traditionally regarded as particularly appropriate for requesting God's pardon, such as during the fast of Ramadan, in preparation for the Haj, during the early morning hours. The hadith and *sunna* of the Prophet, as well as Islamic jurisprudence, prescribe reparations as explicit forms of repentance.[14]

To a large extent, we have focused on monotheistic traditions as settings for dramas of individual-scale repentance and forgiveness. This theater of reconciliation for everyday betrayals and injuries is part of the texture of the religious life and, indeed, of salvation itself. The fissures constantly arising between

---

[14] The most prominent forms of expiation noted are fasting, feeding the hungry, and freeing slaves. For example, see the commentary on the following Qur'anic passages: 2:184, 2:271, 5:89, and 58:3–4 (Nasr et al. 2015).

spouses, within families, and among workers, neighbors, and friends, are, from a faith perspective, constant occasions to revisit this pattern. This widespread activity, however significant to its immediate parties, rarely rises to broader notice unless the cases involve extreme acts, like murder, assault, and abuse.

Is repentance a necessary condition for forgiveness? We find some nuanced differences in emphasis among the monotheistic traditions on this question, as discussed further on. But all affirm that the chronological sequence is not absolute. Forgiveness can sometimes be offered prior to or in the absence of repentance. An example widely publicized in the United States involved a small Amish community in Pennsylvania where a gunman invaded a school and killed five young girls and then himself. The Amish community immediately forgave the assailant (who was beyond the reach of any explicit repentance) and reached out to support his widow and family alongside their own bereaved members (Kraybill, Nolt, and Weaver-Zercher 2007).

Miroslav Volf tells of a friend, abandoned by her alcoholic mother as a small girl, who eventually sought a meeting (Volf 2005: 185–86). Although the child was the one who had been abandoned, she asked forgiveness for never writing or contacting her mother. The mother had been distant and cool during the meeting, but at this, she broke down entirely in a torrent of regret and love toward her daughter. Her shame and guilt had so consumed her that explicit repentance had become impossible until she could actually see forgiveness as a possibility. Forgiveness does not deny wrong. Its very premise is precisely the recognition by forgiver and forgiven alike that a wrong has been committed. But sometimes forgiveness plays a role in eliciting this (actual or explicit) recognition.

The instances just noted operate at the individual scale. It is often harder to disentangle personal hurt and reconciliation from a much-wider social and communal context. This is particularly true when the motivation for the offenses involved is not simply individual but associated with communal identities or with monotheistic traditions themselves. In Northern Nigeria, an area riven with the recent conflict between Muslims and Christians, Pastor James Wuye and Imam Mohammad Ashafa initially played leading roles in organizing their respective communities in violent opposition to each other. They responded to what they saw as aggression from the other side against their religion, their places of worship, and their fellow believers. Bloody battles – in which Imam Ashafa's revered teacher and two of his cousins died and Pastor Wuye lost a hand – left each plotting the death of the other. Their deeply personal grievance was only enhanced by their religious fervor, and each deployed a religious rationale from within their tradition to quiet the same tradition's counsels of forgiveness and peace.

Charged by a mutual acquaintance to meet together as the only two people who could stop the conflagration in their region, they gradually overcame their animosity. The mutual trust between them grew into an organization that worked for reconciliation and harmony among Christians and Muslims ("The Imam and the Pastor" 2008). The Amish example stated before – and similar cases could be found in each tradition – illustrates the way in which a tight-knit monotheistic community provides a formative framework for the individual practice of forgiveness. There is a collective "decisional" certainty that this is the path to be pursued, however difficult it may be to work out in practice. But the Nigerian example illustrates the difficulty when such supportive frameworks for reconciliation of "lower-level" conflicts become themselves parties to the conflict to be resolved. In this case, it is significant that the two traditions can draw on much by way of the shared elements that are described in this section. And yet, in the end, each understands the necessity and the value of their mutual forgiveness in a manner that is particular to their own faith commitment.

This instance also indicates that forgiveness between individuals sometimes reaches far beyond their specific cases and intersects with much larger systems. It is hard to see how the hatred and conflict between communities can be overcome except through the example and leadership of those who become concrete, representative examples of that possibility. Those who have been themselves deeply, directly wounded by the division in question have a unique potential influence when they enter dialogue or model the gift and reception of forgiveness. This is part of the towering stature of Nelson Mandela in the South African context, or the impact of communities of bereaved parents, whether Catholic and Protestant in Northern Ireland or Israeli and Palestinian in the Middle East. We will have occasion to return to this point when we consider intercession later.

2.3.3 Repentance and Law

Repentance and forgiveness interrupt or inflect the connection of justice with retribution, as we otherwise find it. This prompts us to consider the extent to which this apparently deeply personal relation can be socially routinized or administered. The character of grace as a rule-violating excess would seem to preclude its incorporation within a consistent system. But the "injustice" of divine forgiveness has called forth constructive reflections in all the monotheistic theologies. One of these is the vision of purgatory. Those who pass from this life with some claim to have repented (or to have had repentance offered on their behalf) in fact differ wildly in their past behavior and in their present character. That obvious fact leads to a presumption that their forgiveness (and admission to salvation) might be balanced by some process of remediation, whether this is understood as a punishment to purge sin or rehabilitation to fit one for the highest reaches of joy. Purgatory may be specified with the most precision among Christians by Roman Catholic teaching. But the idea of purgation or purification after death is widely shared in the Abrahamic traditions.[15] Islamic tradition specifies an intermediate or "barrier" state between death and the next life, *barzakh*, which some scholars see as similar to purgatory (Yusuf 2015: 1827).

Wherever hell is understood as of limited duration and of a refining effect (for some or all who enter it), the effect is similar. In Judaism, arguably, hell is primarily understood in terms of purification. Such a state, even if it encompasses suffering and struggle, is itself a manifestation of mercy. It represents an alternative to outright annihilation or eternal punishment, and its assured end is a portion in the same glorious state accorded to the most righteous and devout. In it, deferred judgment and deferred beatitude mix and meet. Such a vision can be seen to justify both divine and human forgiveness, since it does not leave sin without effect. Purgatory "administers" forgiveness. It brings offenders up to a level that merits (or is capable of incorporating) the benefits bestowed and implements a kind of justice in distinguishing them from those who did not require purification to the same extent.

Clearly, legal structures developed in the shadow of monotheistic traditions will reflect the fundamental dynamics we have been discussing. In many respects, they parallel thought about purgatory. We call our prisons a "correctional system," or a "penitential system," a term explicitly drawn from a Christian sacramental model where confession, repentance, and absolution (forgiveness) were specific ecclesial rites. The law sets penalties to which criminals are sentenced, a vestige of a "penitential" cost. Instead of leaving retribution in the hands of the injured parties and their relations, we defer to a collective justice system to prescribe something in the nature of involuntary repentance, with a hope that this coerced form of restitution may come to correlate with a sincere attitude of regret and with reformed "good behavior." In return, this routinized repentance will be met with social forgiveness, in the sense of civic restoration to full status within the community. In regard to some offenses, upon fulfillment of certain terms, even the record of the commission of the offense itself will be "wiped clean."

---

[15] That hell is eventually abolished or is only a temporary abode for all its inhabitants is a minority view over the history of Christianity and Islam. Islam knows of intermediate ultimate states (like limbo) and the idea that certain "locations" within hell might serve some as a purgatorial passage to heaven is quite widespread. On Islam and the duration of hell, see Lange 2016: 169–70.

Our western legal systems are rooted historically in religious understandings of repentance and forgiveness. Muslim and Jewish traditions made the connection explicit. They articulated law as a fundamental religious category, in a way that Christianity does not. And this has very much to do with seeing the outworking of the problem of transgression and restoration as part of the divine administration of the world (what Christian theology would call the divine "economy"). The later separation in Christianity between state and church (and later between state and religion) made this question more complex so that the state alone undertook the political, bodily "conciliation" of certain kinds of offenses (and the church claimed no right to such) and the church alone undertook reconciliation of purely spiritual transgressions (which the state excluded from its purview). However, political justice systems did not mean that crimes did not belong also to the ecclesial penitential system: theft or murder required confession, penance, and forgiveness. It was the temporal forms of punishment for these that the church eschewed, not a concern for their significance for the offender's relation to God and their ultimate destiny.

To note this connection is intended not to throw a veil of religious justification over any current justice and prison system, certainly not that in the United States, but to suggest a perspective from which to critique the distorted form of "reconciliation" it may represent. Where social awareness of this legacy is lacking, it is easy to presume a simpler rationale for the justice system. One may regard the system not as an alternative to retribution but precisely as an instrument for it, whose purpose should be to exact at least the same damage to the perpetrator as was visited on the victim. Or one might suppose its role should be solely to institutionalize the application of grace, social forgiveness granted to preempt that from any actual victim. Efforts at "restorative justice" aim to maintain in a legal form some of the same complexity that exists in the religious connection between repentance and renewal (Van Ness and Strong 2010).

The "governance" dimension of mercy and forgiveness bears on *how* God is to be merciful in practical terms, for instance, to determine how much repentance is sufficient to show good faith and how is human law and justice to be organized so as to be consistent with God's gracious nature and yet also with the demands of human life.

There are forms of forgiveness that go beyond the repentance/forgiveness baseline we have just described. God takes initiative to preserve Israel, even when it has disregarded the prophets. God sends the sun and the rain on the just and the unjust alike, regardless of their repentance. There is proactive forgiveness, given even before it is asked, that seems to be a particular divine quality. It is hard to tell where postponement of divine judgment, to give space for repentance or assistance to the offender in actually performing the repentance, bleeds over into frank forgiveness, the "wiping away" of former transgressions. But it is a divine prerogative to take this action.

For instance, a hadith reports that Mohammad once pronounced the death sentence on a murderer, after the killer's family and that of the victim were unable to agree on reparations. His companions saw that he did so with sorrow, and they raised funds to double the restitution that had been offered. When this succeeded and the execution was avoided, the prophet expressed great satisfaction (Sartiprak 2011: 86). Another famous hadith relates to a man who had killed ninety-nine people. The man went to a religious scholar and asked if he could be forgiven. The expert replied, no, your sins are too great. The man flew into a rage and killed the scholar, a hundredth victim. He then went to a mystic and was told you can be forgiven, but you must leave this corrupt place and put yourself in the company of righteous people. The murderer sets out to do this but dies along the way. Two angels come to argue over whether he goes to heaven or hell, by measuring: Was he closer to the point of departure or the new city? He is found closer to the point of departure. But because of the sincerity of the man's repentance, God moves the body until it is just outside the good city. And the man is sent to heaven.[16]

All of the Abrahamic traditions affirm this kind of excess in forgiveness to be characteristic of the divine. Human imitation of God, in this respect, is something they often honor as spiritual attainment, though, as we will see at a later point, it also occasions disagreement over how far it is to be required or commended.

2.3.4 Hard Cases

It is easy to present forgiveness in terms of "happy ending" stories, such as that of the reconciliation between the Nigerian imam and pastor we described earlier. On the scale of lesser daily offenses within relationships of family, friends, and colleagues, such reconciliations are common events. As we will discuss in Section 3, it is questionable whether life would be possible without this dependable dynamic. But the monotheistic case for forgiveness runs up against the monotheistic sense of universal moral order, and sometimes, the two seem impossible to fully reconcile. Even within religious communities, there is nothing like an absolute application of this norm.

For instance, monotheistic communities practice forms of discipline, in which those who violate its standards and are unrepentant are sanctioned or,

---

[16] This *hadith* can be found in the Bukhari collection, Volume 4, Book 55, *hadith* 676. See https://thechoice.one/sahih-al-bukhari-hadith-in-english-all-volumes-1-9/.

at the extreme, expelled from the community. Whether rooted in a concern for the eventual reform of the offending party or a concern to protect the community from corruption, such practices indicate that forgiveness operates contextually, not by a simple rule. All three faiths explicitly consider whether there may be such a thing as an unforgivable sin. In the Jewish tradition blasphemy, defiling the name of God would be the possible candidate. Some Muslims would say that *shirk* (associating another with God) is such (Brown 2016: 15). Christians refer to the sin against the Holy Spirit, for which scripture suggests there can be no pardon (Matthew 12:30–32). Never entirely affirmed, this possibility hovers in the background, a cautionary and sobering shadow.

Simon Wiesenthal wrote a famous book recounting his experience as a Jewish inmate in a German extermination camp during the Holocaust (Wiesenthal, Cargas, and Fetterman 1998). As part of his forced labor, he was sent to a German military hospital to do janitorial work. While there, he was called by a nurse to the bedside of a dying SS soldier who was seeking a Jewish person from whom to ask forgiveness for his earlier participation in a particular act of genocide that now haunted him: the death of some 300 Jews herded into a house that was then burned, while all who tried to escape were shot. The man told Wiesenthal his story, and at its conclusion, Wiesenthal left without saying a word. The next day he learned of the man's death.

In his book, Wiesenthal recounts his own continuing struggle with the question and poses it to the reader: should he have granted forgiveness? The book included some responses to the question from fifty-three prominent religious, philosophical, and public figures. In overwhelming proportion, they said that Wiesenthal should not have granted forgiveness. Only nine of the fifty-three unequivocally advised in favor of it (six Christians and three Buddhists – all the Buddhists who participated), while eight were uncertain. Of those who identified themselves as Jewish, nineteen unequivocally rejected forgiveness in this case, and three were uncertain. Of Christians, six supported forgiveness; five rejected it; and four were uncertain.

The explanations offered by the respondents touched on various considerations. Wiesenthal was being asked to grant forgiveness for acts that were committed against others, and he could/should not speak for them. There was no proof of any true repentance beyond a deathbed self-interest: the confession could no longer pose any dangers to the SS soldier and could only give him subjective relief. The dying soldier was not just someone who had privately committed personally motivated crimes. He had acted in solidarity with a monstrous movement of the evil of much greater scope. To forgive him risked minimizing that evil.

On the other hand, one could not rule out the sincerity of the dying man. Wiesenthal had been sought out and placed in this position because of his membership in a community. Wiesenthal was the sole person in a position to witness to the possibility, if not the certainty, of mercy on the part of the God of his religious tradition. The question was not purely an individual one. His solidarity with his community was at the same time a reason to reject the request – he could not offer absolution on their behalf – and a reason to give him pause – he was being asked to represent, in a sense, the voice of the God that constituted that community.

If hard cases suggest limits to the scope of forgiveness, or at least to the human ability to represent divine mercy, there is an opposite concern, what we might call "pathologies of forgiveness." Alongside questions about forgiveness refused, we can add those about forgiveness granted. For instance, as the sex abuse scandal in the Roman Catholic Church has come to light, it has offered distressing examples of "cheap grace," in which priests guilty of molesting children went through what can be seen clearly in retrospect as the most superficial outward forms of therapeutic and spiritual forgiveness, only to be enabled to continue their abuse in a new location (Globe Newspaper 2002). That many people experience a perceived obligation to forgive, as part of their religious commitment, is something that can be exploited and manipulated by others to escape responsibility and to enable continued abuse or wrongdoing. All traditions recognize that deception and pretense are realities, and feigned repentance is no repentance at all.

Given a common baseline belief in repentance/forgiveness and a shared inclination to honor individuals who may press beyond even that baseline toward an "excess" of forgiveness, monotheists still struggle with the question of limits to forgiveness. This would include the question of whether forgiveness can be separated from sanctions against the offender. Some would suggest that just as true repentance must be expressed in action, so true forgiveness manifests itself by deferring punishment. Can we distinguish social and personal dimensions of mercy, such that one might forgive an offender relationally and still support legal punishment for them? Could I forgive an abuser for their acts toward me, and still desire their incarceration to protect others and even to protect the offender from further guilt and corruption? Most monotheists recognize limits of this sort, areas in which even a saintly individual who desires nothing punitive to be done on their personal account could accept some form of punishment as a restraint on evil. At one extreme might be the case of a person who refuses to press manslaughter charges against a distraught and repentant driver whose tragic inattention led to the death of her child. At the other extreme would be the case of a person who insists on the prosecution of a psychopathic killer who tortured and killed her child and would likely do the same again to others.

Whether we are speaking of interpersonal or social relations, hard cases challenge forgiveness as a religious norm. Though mercy and restoration may be ideal resolutions for all garden variety offenses, and even of great wrongs, can they be so as a prescription for all? When we face the hardest cases, we may hesitate to take God's punishment of evildoers into our own hands, and yet we may not rule out that God will in good time enforce some sanction or some kind of purgation (a kind of required repentance).

2.4 Variations

Many of the doctrinal differences among the Abrahamic faiths relate to variations in the predominant "backstories" of forgiveness provided in each. The same thing can be said often of major divergences within traditions as well (such as those between Protestant and Catholic Christians or between Sunni and Shiite Muslims). Christians have at times claimed Christianity stood above other religions by virtue of its unique concern for forgiveness, mercy, and grace. Such claims ignore the clear teaching and practice in other traditions (not only monotheistic ones, as we have seen) that stress these same points. It is no less common to encounter criticism of Christianity from those in other religious traditions, particularly Judaism and Islam, for a distorted extremity in the Christian approach to forgiveness.

The immoderate claims sometimes made by Christians and the critical observations from other monotheists together suggest that there may be some "outlier" quality to Christianity's profile on these issues and that this may illuminate different emphases among the traditions. I do not mean to suggest that these differences "count" in some way for or against one tradition or another. There are benefits and liabilities in each case, which can be judged finally only in terms of the overall framework of the traditions themselves, and particularly in light of the realizations they envision.[17]

Some key shared elements in the monotheistic approach to forgiveness also can become, in their specification, occasions for divergence among the traditions. We can consider this in terms of *what* it is that requires forgiveness, *who* plays a central role in the process of forgiveness and *how* the forgiveness is

---

[17] For a fuller discussion of this, see Heim 1995.

grounded. In all three instances, the answers turn to some extent on how the traditions conceive the end state on the far side of forgiveness.

2.4.1 What Must Be Forgiven

The existence of a creator God establishes a universal reference for forgiveness. There is one relation in which all humans stand in need of forgiveness. There are numberless persons who I have never met, who have never harmed me nor I them, and with whom no explicit questions of forgiveness arise. But it is a monotheistic assumption that before God, all humans stand in need of this gift. This is not because humans are created evil, intrinsically in need of forgiveness for the very nature of our being. The Abrahamic creator God created humanity good. So the universal need for forgiveness requires some explanation. It entered the story through some combination of "soft dualism" – a tempter, a fallen angel – and human freedom. It is universal in a contingent, not a necessary sense.

In respect to variations on the monotheistic theme, it is useful to note that the problem of forgiveness has a backward-looking dimension (dealing with guilt and memory), a forward-looking dimension (dealing with reconciliation and renewed relation), and what we might call a transitional dimension (the activities and attitudes in the present, pointing in both directions, that bring about the change). In discussing repentance, we touched upon a fundamental common element in this realm of transitional practice. Without repentance, whether it comes early or late, there is no true resolution of the past or path to the future. But other aspects of the picture depend upon how the nature of the past and the future are understood.

For instance, there are variations in the tenor of the story each monotheism tells about the past and the need for human–divine forgiveness. In the Quranic telling of the first sin in Eden, Adam and Eve disobey God and are forced out of the garden by Satan. But this is immediately followed by repentance on their part: "Our Lord! We have wronged ourselves. If Thou dost not forgive us and have mercy upon us, we shall surely be among the losers" (Nasr et al. 2015: 414). God then forgives them. So this first story is also the first instantiation of the sin-repentasnce-forgiveness pattern as the resolution of transgression, though it is also clear that humanity lives now in an environment different from the original garden. In the Jewish and Christian Bibles, there is more suggestion that the disobedience and expulsion (by God) from the garden alter not only the external conditions under which humanity lives but also the character of human relations with each other and with God. God has ratified certain consequences to the disobedience: estrangements among humans and between humans and creation.

All three traditions reflect a tension between understanding the advent of disobedience as the initiation of a *pattern* in human–divine relations, in which forgiveness on the basis of repentance is the gracious and consistent divine role, and understanding it as corruption in the human *medium* through which these relations are formed. In the latter case, the passing over of specific offenses is not necessarily a sufficient solution. In the first understanding, the need for forgiveness of specific behaviors is a continually renewed circumstance. In the second, it is a universal propensity or condition – a rewriting or rewiring of the very relation between God and humanity – that is at issue.

Some Christians came to characterize this second understanding with the title "original sin." This is a misleading term. It is precisely not "original," in the sense of being part of initial creation, but a subsequent and contingent development. It is "original" practically speaking, in that all humans *now* start with a legacy of distortion in the human relation with God. It is not intrinsic in the creation and will not be characteristic of redeemed humanity, but it is the gravitational field around any of our actual choices or acts. For the purposes of our discussion here, this is relevant in the backward-looking sense that forgiveness for past acts or events does not address the previously acquired (and continuing) condition. It is relevant in the forward-looking sense that true reconciliation will require some change in that reality. And it is relevant in the current, transitional assessment of what in us is the proper material for pardon or mercy. Does this include things that are more structural and attitudinal – privilege or benefit at another's expense, envy, or indifference in our inner spirits – as well as those that are decisional and behavioral? In other words, what counts as something in need of mercy and reconciliation?

This is an index to the extremity many Jewish and Muslim observers find in Christian approaches. Christian views on sin may give rise to additional things for which forgiveness or restoration may be needed: a condition we do not ourselves create but participate in (harkening back to the corporate dimension of sin we saw in some biblical sources) and/or thoughts and desires that constitute offenses, even if they do not eventuate in actual acts (lust and pride). In these respects, Christians have tended to push out the borders of the territory where forgiveness should be applied, to an extent not necessarily endorsed by others.[18]

This extension of the scope of forgiveness could be seen both as setting a higher bar for judgment and as introducing more extenuating circumstances (in a condition that cannot be remediated solely by repentance). We normally

---

[18] In some ways, this "extension" leads more deeply into the area of negative emotions where we saw Buddhist analysis centered its understanding of forbearance.

think of forgiveness as a response to acts. It is more complicated in relation to desires and intent. This is something like the difference between forgiving behavior and forgiving a person. The more we love a person, the easier it may be to forgive their behavior. But what kind of redemption is it where one is forgiven, only to need the same forgiveness again and again indefinitely? What kind of relation is possible with such a person? An acceptance of the "offense-generating" person, a forgiveness of the person as such, is a prospective act, an acceptance in the knowledge of future sins yet uncommitted. This is a different kind of "excess" divine mercy, an acceptance of the sinner as such.

To Muslims and Jews, emphasis on this form of forgiveness can tend to overpower the requirements relating to act-specific forgiveness, resulting in a kind of license to bypass repentance altogether in expectation of a comprehensive pardon. As one Jewish scholar observed, "Not all Christian spiritual mentors teach that forgiveness should be granted in the absence of repentance, and not all Jewish spiritual ones teach that repentance must always be a prerequisite to forgiveness," but this does not change the fact that the inclinations in each community differ (Schimmel 2002: 83).

Both Muslim and Jewish commentators show particular concern that the Christian understanding of sin (specifically of "original sin") has overstepped, turning the distinction between God and creation into a chasm, one that requires extraordinary activities or assumptions to bridge (assumptions like incarnation, atonement, and Trinity). This verges on a presumptuous discontent with the sufficiency of the repentance/forgiveness dynamic itself, a discontent that seeks a more profound transformation of the human and a presumption that ventures even to count the costs of reconciliation on God's part.

2.4.2 Intercession

Forgiveness is rooted in the free choice by God to treat repentance as a sufficient basis for deferral of punishment and restoration of relation. We saw that the signals of true repentance could include restitution to victims, acts of "excess" good to others, and acts of self-denial on the part of the offender. Such acts of repentance could be considered as a making whole of what had been divided, reconciling those that transgression has put at odds. Such acts do not themselves alone produce forgiveness, apart from the prior choice of God to treat them in this vein, just as they cannot produce peace among human parties apart from the concurrence of the injured party.

God's willingness to forgive based upon repentance sets a kind of lower boundary but not a ceiling. It does not rule out the divine expression of excess mercy even by reference to this standard. If we ask what "funds" the repentance/forgiveness itself and what may be the occasion of grace given even in the absence of any initiative from the offender, we should add another element to the picture: intercession. Repentance necessarily involves a direct admission of wrong and a direct request for mercy. In monotheistic terms, this is always a three-party act, and the admission and plea go both to the victim and to God. Request for mercy (from the human victim and/or from God) on the part of someone other than the offender is an intercession.

In the book of Genesis, Abraham bargains successfully with God over the threatened destruction of the city of Sodom (Genesis 18:22–33). Abraham objects to God that it would be wrong to kill the righteous along with sinners, and God replies that if only fifty righteous (eventually reduced to ten) are found in the city, he will spare the entire population for their sakes. Here, we see a plea for mercy that bypasses the offenders themselves, a request made on their behalf by someone who does not share their offense. In this case, leniency is requested in the interests of justice: the innocent should not be "collateral damage" in the punishment of the offenders. Abraham raises this argument, and presumably, God accepts it partly because of its moral cogency and partly because it is made by an upright and merciful person.

There is no clear connection between avoiding harm to the innocent, in the midst of justified punishment of the wicked, and extending grace to offenders because of the virtues of those who appeal on their behalf. The prophets plead for their people, appealing to the "excess" in God's loving-kindness, at the same time that they may also themselves offer a kind of representative penance on behalf of the nation or act out their trust in God's redemptive purpose. The prophetic role of warning people of their sins is often complemented with a reciprocal petition to God on behalf of the erring people. In Islamic tradition, Mohammad is an intercessor of this sort, the one whose extraordinary closeness to God enhances the effect of his petitions. An intercessor is not a primary party in the "triangle" of offender-victim-God. She acts by virtue of her standing with God on the one hand and by virtue of her caring connection with the victim and the offender on the other, as a participant in and a voice from the wider community around their reconciliation.

God is an offended party in all sin. And, by honoring or appointing intercessors, God has actually become an intercessor, on behalf of offenders against God and on behalf of offenders in relation to their human victims. There is a pattern here, in which God occupies at once in different respects the roles of victim, intercessor, and judge. Each of the traditions stretches this pattern into its own distinctive shapes.

Earlier we discussed monotheistic views on *what* it is that requires forgiveness. Consideration of intercession demonstrates that there is also a crucial element related to *who* figures in the granting of it. We noted the monotheistic agreement that forgiveness is always a three-party process. We can now see that typically it is in fact wider: it may include intercessors or even a community of/ as intercessors. Just as certain places or times may enhance repentant requests for pardon and spark new inclinations to offer mercy, so too may the voice of certain persons commending this reconciliation. Those in search of forgiveness can appeal not only to God and to those directly injured by their acts but also to others to commend that appeal to the principal parties. In this respect, the traditions are distinguished by primary appeal to different intercessor figures: Mohammad would be widely seen in such a way by Muslims. Saints would be seen so by many Christians. Some figures, such as Jesus and Mary, the mother of Jesus, might figure, in both traditions, though not to the same degree. Typically, in Judaism, it is the entire community that most often features an intercessory role. Disagreement over preferred or legitimate intercessor figures, as well as the mode of intercession, can be a significant factor in denominational differences within traditions.

Cost of Repentance and Intercession

Repentance includes a dimension of suffering on the part of the offender. The moral effort, sacrifice of resources, and subjective pain involved in penitential behavior are forms of redemptive suffering, in that these are applied toward the end of achieving forgiveness and restoration. Just as suffering can be an attendant dimension of true repentance, it is sometimes a feature of intercession as well. The intercessor not only speaks on behalf of those in need of forgiveness but offers a kind of repentance on their behalf as well. Thus, Daniel fasted in sackcloth and ashes and prayed in repentance to God, not for his peculiar personal faults but on behalf of the people: "we have sinned and done wrong, and acted wickedly and rebelled, turning aside from thy commandments and ordinances" (Daniel 9:5). This voice of collective confession, seeking a kind of collective forgiveness, became a common feature of liturgy and worship, alongside individual confession.

Suffering can be a kind of qualification for an intercessor, intensifying the value of their prayers for others. The Shi'ite branch of Islam is particularly notable in this respect. The Imams, the true lineal and spiritual descendants of the prophet, are intercessors of supreme power, and this power derives in large measure from the fact of their suffering in the cause of God (Ayoub 1978: 198–205). In a different sense, the "righteous remnant" of those within Israel who remain faithful in the face of trial preserve the hope of redemption for the entire community. The intercession of the righteous is of great value and that of those who suffer for the right, even more so.

Intercessors typically amplify the repentance and apology offered first-hand by offenders. But, as the example from Abraham indicates, they introduce the possibility of forgiveness being granted without actual repentance or request· from the primary parties. The wicked who would be spared on Abraham's request have made none of their own. They are not even aware of his intercession on their behalf. Prophets who preach repentance often also assume a promissory role – assuring their people that God will certainly and quickly offer forgiveness to those who seek it. Here, the prophet comes close to announcing future forgiveness to those who have not (yet) asked for it, the assurance being a strong part of the motivation to repent. The prophet mediates a promise or announcement of forgiveness to those it is not his own place to pardon. Rather than enhancing the request on behalf of another, the prophet conveys the response on behalf of God.

In these respects, the basic grammar of offender and victim has become quite complex. Our discussion of intercession leads finally to the possibility of proactive forgiveness. An injured party may act to forgive, even in the absence of repentance on the part of the guilty. In such a case, the person has become an intervenor in their own case so to speak, advocating on behalf of the offender as a kind of intercessor victim, who forgives unilaterally. From the monotheistic perspective, this behavior makes sense not simply as a sacrificial effort to redeem the other, to provide what they may not have the means to seek themselves (or what may be impossible for them – as for instance if they have died), but as part of the actor's own life in communion with God. This level of intercession on behalf of another, an enemy other, becomes also a form of witness and testimony to God. This was very much the case in a widely publicized case in the United States, where family members of those killed in a racially motivated shooting at a Black church service appeared just days later at a hearing for the murderer to state their forgiveness.[19] This expression of faith did not wait upon the action of the killer (who in fact did not express repentance).

Here forgiving becomes "fore-giving," an act in advance of what are thought to be its normal preconditions (Liechty 2006: 62). Repentance becomes not a precondition for but a "necessary result or consequence of

---

[19] See ABC News 2015.

divine forgiveness (Karkkainen 2016: 7)." Among Christians, Protestants are notable for affirming unconditional divine forgiveness, for which human repentance is a mode of acceptance of this grace and not a prior condition for it. But Christians in general lean in this direction as compared to most of their monotheistic neighbors. The frequency and confidence with which Christians often express assurance that divine forgiveness is an accomplished fact strike many as a kind of antinomianism. That is, it is an attitude that could downplay repentance and encourage people to sin repeatedly, in trust that they are already absolved.

In part, this Christian inclination rests on the example of Jesus, who in the New Testament (even from the cross at his death) offers forgiveness without prior proof of repentance, and on the interpretation of Jesus's message by the apostle Paul, who announces that God offered forgiveness in Christ "while we were yet sinners" (Romans 5:8). But in a more general sense, it relates to the topic of intercession. We have seen that intercession complicates the traditional forgiveness "triangle" of offender-victim-God. The Christian understanding of Christ's role presses intercession into a distinctive shape.

The efforts expended by a repentant offender, in restitution or atonement, can be seen as a kind of sacrifice offered in the interests of atoning for their sin. The suffering and concern of a "third-party" intercessor, seeking reconciliation between offender and victim, can likewise be seen as a kind of redemptive suffering. Christian tradition has developed the role of God as intercessor in a particular way, linking the free, proactive forgiveness of sinners to a sacrificial gift on God's part, offered through God's incarnation in Jesus.

Christianity stresses the cost of divine grace, affirming that God has literally become a suffering intercessor, wounded by the same sin for which mercy is sought. Christians describe God as constitutively complex, in whom three modes of existence coinhere as one reality: Trinity. Unnecessary (if not offensive) to Jews and Muslims, this conviction "works" for Christians both to express the dynamic in which God can identify and act as intercessor, victim, and judge at once and to suggest the basis for a particular sort of intimacy in the nature of final reconciliation, an almost "psychological" characteristic of that reconciliation. My interest here is only to point out how key elements that Jews and Muslims typically find objectionable in Christianity (incarnation and Trinity) can be seen to arise from divergences in approach to forgiveness: supposition of an event basis for forgiveness (in the incarnation, death, and resurrection of Christ) and concern for participation in the inner divine life as part of ultimate reconciliation.

2.4.3 Forgiveness and Atonement

Atonement 1: What Makes Forgiveness Possible?

"Atonement" is an ambiguous word. It can point to the state of being reconciled (the end point of a particular repentance/forgiveness process) or to the state of ultimate reconciliation and unity of humans with God and each other on the other side of all repentance and forgiveness (essentially the same as salvation). It is also used (especially in its verbal form – "atoning") to refer to actions within the process of repentance and pardon, specifically the actions that involve "making up" for what was done or offering as a gift something valuable but different from what was lost. That is to say, the word can indicate both the condition that forgiveness makes possible and the actions that make forgiveness possible. A third, and typically Christian, use makes the noun a proper title for a singular event that is the basis for the other two meanings: the event of God's incarnation in Jesus Christ and the atonement of divine and human natures. In some veins of Christianity, the reference is narrower. The vast scope of God's mercy in lifting condemnation from sinners is "justified" to use Paul's language in Romans 3, by a counterbalancing and unmerited condemnation accepted by Christ. It is Jesus's death on the cross that is the specific event of atonement that corresponds to God's forgiveness of human sin.[20]

If we ask what makes forgiveness possible, the monotheistic faiths are in profound agreement that it is rooted in the fundamental nature of God. The relevant defining divine quality – grace or love – is much wider and richer than merely forsaking retaliation. Creation itself can be seen as expressing this mercy, sympathy, and love for what is less and other than God. A hadith holds that if there had been no sin in this world, God would have created another, in order to be able to forgive.[21] Miroslav Volf points to a rabbinical story to the same effect (Volf 2005: 136). God foresaw the misdeeds of humanity and considered that the world about to be created would in justice have to be destroyed unless it could be forgiven. The very act of creation itself was founded on grace and on anticipated mercy. At one level, the exercise of

---

[20] The "penal substitutionary" view of Christ's death holds that it offered "atonement" (action of compensation for sins) on behalf of humanity. For our purposes here, it is important simply to note that this view is not identical with Christianity itself. There is no creedal orthodoxy on the "how" of Christ's saving work or the role of the cross in it (as there is on Christ's person or the trinitarian nature of God). The penal substitutionary view has never been prominent in the Eastern Christian church and has always been intertwined with other views in the Western church. For more, see Heim 2006.

[21] A hadith found in Sahih Muslim, Book 37, Hadith 6622. See Muslim 2020. Abu Huraira reported Allah's Messenger having said: "By Him in Whose Hand is my life, if you were not to commit sin, Allah would sweep you out of existence and He would replace (you by) those people who would commit sin and seek forgiveness from Allah, and He would have pardoned them."

grace is simply an expression of the contrast between God and creatures, an example of what makes God different from us, to begin with. Heinrich Heine gave a somewhat flippant expression to this idea with his famous deathbed statement, "God will forgive me; it's His job" (Freud and Crick 2002: 109).

To refer the explanation to this final source forcibly raises the question of how justice and mercy both can reside in the same ultimate. Monotheisms converge in ascribing to God the power to overcome what seems irreparable harm. In this sense, monotheistic faiths all include an eschatological explanation of what makes forgiveness possible. But these traditions agree that things have not (yet) been made entirely right. There is much in need of an eschatological adjustment. This is part of the reason that people can forgive: they can leave this unresolved dimension in God's hands. The backward-looking task of dealing with wrongs is not finished. It is the divine consummation of history and the final dispositions of divine judgment that will underwrite the apparent inequities involved in people being spared the consequences of their behavior. Acts of forgiveness that have gone unrequited in history, in that they were not redeemed by evident outcomes of reconciliation and new life, will nonetheless prove to have been both valuable and justified.

All three traditions recognize that the offer of divine forgiveness is at the same time itself the delivery of divine judgment, part of the eschatological reckoning that flows into the present. All pardon makes explicit the wrong involved. God, in forgiving, is in the same act the vindicator and advocate for victims (ratifying the reality of the hurt done to them) and the prosecutor of the offenders (recognizing their offense and requiring confession of it). No one can accept forgiveness without placing themselves in the wrong. Proactive intercession and mercy are good news only to those who can accept that it is addressed to them, who can fully accept the judgment against them.

The prospect of the last judgment may be the final temporal reference point that grounds forgiveness, short of the divine nature itself. But there are also more practical, immediate, and instrumental answers to the question. In history, there is a program in place for dealing with sin. It is made up of some combination of all the factors of repentance we have reviewed – regret, confession, restitution, expiation, intercession, and gratuitous gift – and it leads to forgiveness. In each of the Abrahamic traditions, there are distinctive frameworks that make these generic points concrete. Belief in divine forgiveness is not an abstract concept. It is based on and clothed in specific forms. For a Jew, trust in divine forgiveness is inseparable from God's covenant relation with Israel and with humanity, to which God will remain faithful even when humans fail. For a Christian, the conviction of God's forgiving grace is inseparable from faith in Christ as the living Word of God. For a Muslim, confidence in God's mercy is inseparable from recognition of the Qur'an as a definitive communication of God's nature and will.

The constellation of these historical factors is different among the monotheistic traditions and varies also within them. For instance, it is clear that the Christian view of Christ and Christ's role presses the idea of an intercessor to a point unusual if not unacceptable for the other traditions. Christ is a universal intercessor for all. And if an intercessor's effect is magnified by their righteous suffering and unity with God, then Christian doctrine makes Christ the supreme combination of both of these. At the same time, the view of Christ's work pushes the idea of expiation to an unusual extent, stretching it to apply not to acts that cancel one's own transgressions or even to the vicarious repentance offered by third-party intercessors on behalf of specific others but to the gift of a single life offered for all.

Within all three traditions, there are controversies over "works and grace," over whether or to what extent those who fulfill the expectations of repentance have earned forgiveness. And all three agree in principle that whatever "system" God has introduced already incorporates mercy as its premise. Jews and Muslims often maintain that Christians slight or even ignore some of the expectations of the repentance process and lean too much toward proactive and even unilateral kinds of forgiveness. So, for instance, when confession and penance are dealt with in a liturgical way in the church, there is no conception that the prescribed actions themselves (a week of fasting, say, for an act of violence) in any respect "wipe away" or expiate the offenses. It is presumed that these activities draw upon another source of reconciliation, another basis for forgiveness, given in the incarnation. In other words, the traditions diverge somewhat – and Jews and Muslims tend to agree particularly that Christians diverge – over the full account of the *basis* for God's exercise of this mercy. This conversation goes hand in hand with the suggestion outlined earlier (Section 2.4.1) that there might be a difference in the scope of what it is that needs to be forgiven or healed.

In Section 1, we compared Buddhist and Christian parables of the "prodigal son." We can return to this example here. From the middle ages, this parable has been a particular favorite in Muslim critiques of Christianity (Bailey 1998: 34). Islamic writers observed that the father in the story, who plainly stands for God, responds directly and immediately to the erring child. They often quoted a hadith of Mohammad as a direct parallel to the parable. In it, Mohammad conveys a message from God: "Whoever comes to me walking, I will come to them running" (Sartiprak 2011: 78). Nothing more is needed: there is no intermediary or intercessor involved, no atoning action as a condition for the parent to act in this gracious manner.

In Jesus's parable, in other words, there is no place for the very role that Christians attribute to Jesus, as the reconciling act of God. The wayward child had repented sufficiently to turn again toward home and had prepared a confession of error, even if they were embraced before delivering it. The basic elements of the repent-and-forgive paradigm had been fulfilled. Seeing this, the parent raced to accept the prodigal. As with any act of divine sovereignty, it is enough that God says "let it be," and it is so. The human need is for sufficient ground to trust and act on the assumption that this truly is God's nature and will – authority like the communication revealed in the Qur'an or the revelation to Israel of God's covenantal faithfulness.

To put it another way, Muslim and Jewish thinkers do not regard the constellation of repentance-related factors we have described as alternatives to grace. Their provision and acceptance already *are* the grace that has been provided, representing a merciful condescension on God's part. Christians have a tendency to contrast law with mercy and to lose touch with the profound sense in which Jewish and later Muslim traditions understand the law *as* grace. This is particularly true of the practices of ritual law in Jewish tradition, observances that serve no obvious moral or utilitarian purpose. This fits them all the better to be a language of intimacy between God and God's people, whose end is that relation itself. Law is given not mainly as a test by which humanity may be found wanting, but as a guide to the fullness of life.

Even more pertinent to our topic, the law contains itself the corrective to violations or failures. "Return" is the refrain of the biblical prophets – return to obedient observance of the commandments. There are important distinctions in law (in this case, perhaps most explicitly delineated in Islam) between what is obligatory and forbidden on the one hand and on the other hand between what is simply allowed and what is praiseworthy in an "over and above" sense. This provides the basis for a form of expiation, where virtuous but not obligatory acts can wipe away failures in obligation or violations of prohibitions. Observance of the law is its own repair of a breach of the law, and the standard of the law defines the path of repentance.

We noted earlier that in the Qur'an, forgiveness followed immediately upon Eve and Adam being driven out of Eden by Satan and their confession of error. It is a common belief in Islamic tradition that the sincere profession of the *Shahādah,* the Muslim confession of faith in God alone and Mohammad as God's messenger, "corrects virtually the effect of the fall" (Glassé 1989: 23). Forgiveness by itself is not a perfect "reset" mechanism, but in association with restoration of the right attitude toward God, it can be. Furthermore, the Qur'an firmly endorses the principle of expiation of bad acts by supererogatory good ones, prescribing a fast, the feeding of a certain number of hungry people, or the freeing of a slave as an equivalent for a given offense. A saying of Mohammad advises "When you perform an evil deed, follow it with a good deed and it will wipe it away" (Nasr et al. 2015: 118).

The differences among the monotheisms that we have described are differences over the *form* in which they identify and experience the assurance of forgiveness, rooted in the divine nature and choice. This assurance comes primarily through Hebrew, Christian, or Muslim scriptures. It is testified to by different events (Israel's return from exile, Mohammad's treatment of his defeated enemies, and Christ's forgiveness of those who crucify him). It is granted in reference to different key intercessors (the prophets, Mohammad, Christ, and other righteous ones and saints). It is administered or confirmed through the sacramental or legal modalities of different religious communities (derived from rabbinic, ecclesial, or shariah sources).

These differences can, at some point, become not a difference in the form the assurance of forgiveness takes but a disagreement over the instrumental *basis* for God's offering the forgiveness. At the final judgment, Islamic tradition says that Mohammad is a universal intercessor for all humanity. Would forgiveness be possible apart from that intercession? Christians say that Christ died for all. Is this a necessary instrumentality without which divine forgiveness would not be granted as it is? God's faithfulness to the covenants God made with all people in Noah, and particularly to the covenant with Israel, is the internal ground for divine mercy, according to Jewish tradition. Without that covenant, would the other intercessors be in vain? While the parable of the prodigal illustrates the agreed root cause of forgiveness in God's own will, other New Testament parables highlight another aspect. The parable of the vineyard, for instance, tells of an owner who sends an emissary to collect rent from his tenants, only to have the servant beaten and driven away (Matthew 21:33–46). Rather than punishing the tenants, the owner sends further messengers who are also mistreated, and finally sends their own child, whom the tenants kill. Passing over transgression can have a terrible cost. And the cost is likely highest if it is precisely the most unrepentant and defiant that one seeks to forgive. Even the "happy ending" parable of the prodigal ends with discord still in view, where the reconciliation of parent and returning child has alienated the older brother because of perceived disparate treatment. These Christian sources stress a thread of divine travail in the exercise of mercy, and intimate that God pays a price to forgive.

The components of expiation and intercession common to the traditions already involve recognition of a certain "cost," a certain condescension for God, who bends to accept repentance instead of strict justice, to respond to intercessors as well as to the primary actors themselves. The way that each develops their understanding of this has something to do with where they see this entire process leading. The full job description for what mercy must get done depends somewhat on the imagined endpoint, the specific character of the expected salvation. That is what we will take up in the following section.

Atonement 2: What Does Forgiveness Make Possible?

Forgiveness has two outcomes, one proximate and historical, the other ultimate. The first, a "foretaste" of redemption, is made up of the concrete reconciliation and new beginnings that the practice of mercy episodically achieves in history. This is critical for our capacity to build through and beyond our failures. If human social life as a whole is to progress closer to God's purpose and if our individual personalities are to be remade closer to the divine image, these events of grace and peacemaking – imperfect and impermanent as their healed divisions maybe – are necessary components. The second, more definitive, outcome is the attainment of God's desired end for creation. This is doubly a "post-forgiveness" condition, one that forgiveness has made possible but in which it is no longer needed to overcome estrangement among creatures or between creatures and God.

In human history, there seems no reason to expect any end to the constant cycle of transgression that requires repentance, repentance that may warrant and receive forgiveness, and forgiveness granted that is followed in turn by new transgressions. The capacity to seek and grant pardon from each other marks moral and emotional maturity. For the monotheistic traditions, growth in this capacity is a mark of holiness. Looking backward, forgiveness does not change facts but affects the guilt, memory, and continuing effects associated with them. The realities of history and of moral judgment are not abolished. Their meanings are altered so that guilt and shame are disarmed from doing further harm. This is not the same as saying time passively heals wounds. Something active must be done, ideally on the part of all parties, so that what was a past wrong with its hurt has become the same wrong and hurt, now included in a story of reconciliation and peace. The plot of which these were a part has been changed.

Forgiveness provides a "clean slate." But is this resolution ever anything but temporary among us or between God and humanity? Looking forward, if forgiveness is to lead to permanent reconciliation between God and humanity, it seems it must lead to a state where forgiveness is no longer necessary, a state where humanity no longer commits offenses that require forgiveness and where past offenses are no longer a barrier to unity with each other and with God because of unresolved injustice or estrangement.

In this light, we can distinguish two separate meanings for the word. The first we can call reparative forgiveness. It denotes a discrete event/act of forgiveness and its outcome, of the sort that must be repeated in succession in the same relationships and taken up anew in fresh ones. The new normal, established in the wake of division and betrayal, is always fragile to new disruption. The harder the case, the less likely that this new normal is fully satisfactory in an ultimate sense. Reparative forgiveness enables a different kind of future, with respect to the specific transgression involved, but does not guarantee it. It certainly does not expect or provide an end to all offenses.

Abrahamic faiths treat the practice of reparative forgiveness as a kind of interim activity that is "funded" eschatologically by the prospect of a final, reconciling forgiveness. Everything in the human practice of forgiveness that does not empirically "pay its way" to the foreseeable practical satisfaction of all the parties is referred for some further final adjustment through the divine agency. Reconciled forgiveness refers to a definitive state of atonement or restoration in which persons or relationships have been accepted comprehensively, an acceptance in which any residual unsatisfactoriness in specific past acts of reparative mercy, and all fragility in their achievements are removed.

The closest analogy for this we can imagine would be the rare and dramatic stories of human forgiveness, where the reconciliation of two persons has become a source of unexpected joy and blessing in their lives and a constant impetus toward good in the lives of others. This is the sort of pardon that would be granted in the final judgment. It does not so much allow a different future as announce and embody it. The acceptance recognizes a change not in the meaning of a past event but in the structure of the relation. The reconciliation involved here has the character of unity of spirit and will, such that the alienation that is the germ of transgression is absent going forward, and so too is the need for mercy.

All monotheists would agree that the final condition is one where there will be no future need for reparative forgiveness. The Qur'an says that in paradise "They hear no idle talk therein, nor incitement to sin, save that 'Peace, peace!' is uttered" (Surah 56:25–26). The prophet Isaiah's vision was the same: "They shall not hurt or destroy in all my holy mountain, for the earth shall be full of the knowledge of the Lord, as the waters cover the sea" (Isaiah 111:9). Visions of this final state vary in several respects, including the degree to which they picture a perfected historical realm or a frankly other-worldly "new creation."

That this state is one of perfected love and obedience, all also agree. What this means diverges according to the understanding of divine and human natures. In some cases, the perfected relation tends strongly toward unity, even a kind of identity. In others, the perfection preserves and honors the absolute distance between the creator and the creature. This variation exists within each tradition to some extent. Thus, Sufi Muslims typically conceive of ultimate reconciliation with God in terms suggestive of unity, while most Muslims would think paradise a reward that completes human nature but one that still observes, even more perfectly than on earth, the distinction from divine transcendence above it.

Forgiveness between humans, and certainly between God and humans, is entirely compatible with the parties to the same forgiveness having quite different perspectives on it. "It is over and done with." "Don't think about it any more." "Let's go forward." These are appropriate and admirable voices of forgiveness. But they are hard to maintain as sufficient, the deeper the wound and the more intimate the ongoing relation. The felt reality of continuing loss for the victim and their awareness of the way repentance falls short of true restoration – these cannot be known in the same way by the penitent. Likewise, even a reconciled offender may continue to be wounded by the fact of their offense and by regret that it cannot be made fully right – experiences not fully known by the victim. This inability to fully inhabit each other's experience is perhaps crucial to the imperfect reconciliations we achieve in history. Without this blindness, we would regularly be derailed either by our disappointment at the inner shallowness of our counterpart's commitment or by our despair at their continued pain. But how are such things to be dealt with in the state of ultimate reconciliation, if that is a condition of full mutual knowledge and shared joy?

This need for a "healing of memory" remains the unresolved open wound in historical forgiveness. A double bind applies to forgiven sinners, one only intensified by the elevated spiritual condition of the redeemed. Precisely to the extent they have become righteous, such persons will always be troubled by the awareness of their past offenses and their inability to have offered any adequate recompense. If they are not troubled by this, they may be happy, but they will never be truly good. Insofar as they have become good enough to have this concern, they can never be truly happy.[22]

There is no canonical resolution of this question in the monotheistic traditions. Some hold that in the blessed state there could be no true joy except through amnesia, in which the doing of justice will be crowned by erasing awareness of any painful past. Full reconciliation would have the effect of canceling out even the recollection of reparative forgiveness. The memory of pain, as a spur both to justice and reconciliation, is no longer needed, and so is itself an evil to be removed. The happiness of the new life is perfect only in the

---

[22] This point is made by Saint Anselm in *Cur Deus Homo, Book I, XXIV.*

obliteration of the old through the "grace of nonremembering" (Volf 1996: 138). In a like manner, some suggested that the redeemed should be held ignorant of any kind of excellence or joys other than their own, lest they be distressed by negative comparison with others.[23]

Some believe that even for the horrors of history, perpetrators and victims may be reconciled in a state where the memory of these realities is not entirely lost, where they know each other still with some narrative sense of those histories. If final joy is constituted from the diversity of identities and gifts of creatures, rather than their abolition, then forgiveness would play its role in those identities. The evil committed and the pain endured would remain in some sense as that out of which divine love has redeemed and healed us. Final reconciliation, thus, would achieve what reparative forgiveness can only dimly suggest.

The end state looks somewhat different in these visions, according to the manner that God and persons are present in these states. The more profound the intimacy of the divine and the human, and the more that memory remains constitutive to identities and relations, the higher the bar is set for reconciliation. We might say the deeper the union or communion, the greater the task that reconciling forgiveness must achieve, extending deep into the shared interiority of the participants. It must satisfy not so much an abstract standard of justice, as the hope for a shared immediate awareness between the reconciled parties that works out to unqualified joy and gratitude. If the end is to raise humanity to a level worthy and capable of proportional human felicity, then it is a matter of God implementing the proper standard for that achievement. If final, reconciling forgiveness involves participation in the divine life, this suggests something rather different, an intimacy with the divine being. In both cases what we are talking about is the afterlife of forgiveness, the nature of the relation it constitutes. Once this afterlife has been achieved, how does God live with God's self while living with forgiven sinners, and how do those forgiven ones live with themselves, each other, and with God?

2.5 Summary

We have seen that monotheistic faith provides a universal moral standard by which to define the need for forgiveness, at the same time that it affirms a shared human need for forgiveness from God as well as from particular parties. The result is a common "grammar" regarding repentance and forgiveness, reflected in our perspectives on law and justice. Monotheistic traditions vary within and among themselves in regard to specifics about intercession and intercessors, the

---

[23] The Muslim author Ibn-arabi is an example. See Asín Palacios and Sunderland 1968: 159.

costs of repentance and intercession, the basis in salvation history for divine mercy, and the nature of the final state of reconciliation.

3 Forgiveness and Human Community

> Only humans can perform that most unnatural act [of forgiveness] which transcends the relentless law of nature.
>
> Alexander Solzhenitsyn (Yancey 1997: 98)

3.1 Forgiveness in the Human Story

In its modest, most routinized forms, forgiveness is a constant feature of our daily lives, sometimes fading into mere courtesy: "Don't mention it." In its most extreme instances, forgiveness is an extraordinary behavior, testing the limits of what seems humanly possible, wise, or just. Solzhenitsyn suggests that forgiveness is a defining feature of humanity, an unnatural act that transcends the law of nature. But how far may the reset dynamic of forgiveness be *part* of that "relentless law of nature," as well as something that pushes beyond it?

In this final section, I explore the connection of our subject with evolutionary history. I do so to put the basic information reviewed so far in a different light and to indicate that religious practices of forgiveness, in both extraordinary and everyday manifestations, are profoundly integral to the development of our humanity. Some practice of non-retaliation features in normal biological life as part of the economy of nature. And part of what made us human was a specifically religious extension of this feature. This "excess" in forgiveness, an economy of grace, became part of the peculiar character of emergent human nature.

The benefits of forgiveness are most often pictured as healing for individual victims and offenders. We less often discuss forgiveness given or received by subjects other than individuals (such as communities or groups) or the role of forgiveness in constituting communities.[24] This section deals with forgiveness relative to the constitution of human communities and the constitution of the "community" of humanity itself.

Monotheism points us in this direction by giving forgiveness a universal formulation, treating it as a fundamental structural concern, as well as a contingent and personal one. In previous sections, we assessed forgiveness primarily by its effects within the forgiver, within the forgiven, or in the relation between them. But the role of forgiveness can be measured also as a function of an entire system or as a condition for certain kinds of community.

---

[24] We saw, in our brief discussion of forgiveness and law, that the subject certainly extends into these areas.

The benefit of forgiveness to individuals cannot be divorced from its value in redeeming relationships. If the practice of forgiveness at times evades clear resolution of questions of justice, it suffers that tension in the interests of allowing a relationship to begin anew or to be maintained. We readily understand the desire for conciliation among those in tight-knit groups. The more integral, unavoidable, and previously valued the connections, the more interest we have in maintaining or redeeming them. The more ephemeral and contingent the bond, the less investment attaches to forgiveness.

Apart from any subjective, inner peace that may be attained, it is the relation, as a distinct reality in its own right, that is saved and kept operational. In this respect, "paired" forgiveness becomes a matter in which others who belong to a network around the parties also have an investment. Forgiveness is often urged by third parties in these terms.[25] For them, the health of the entire web of relations, encompassing both offender and victim, counts for a great deal. Conversely, if others in this web insist upon a rupture in relations between the immediate parties, the cost of forgiveness for the victim escalates dramatically to include the risk of wider losses distinct from those imposed by the injury itself.

3.2 Forgiveness as Altruism

A social perspective on forgiveness emerges from debates over altruism within the study of human evolutionary development. To recognize the connection, we need to reconceive forgiveness as a particular kind of altruism. In evolutionary terms, altruism means one organism gives up a fitness benefit (something material or positional that that would foster the health/status and reproductive success of that organism and its genes) in favor of another organism that receives the benefit instead. The sacrifice is classically material: the loss of food, shelter, or mating opportunities that are transferred to another. We can conceive of forgiveness as another modality of altruism, where what is given up is not something positive but something defensive: retaliation and self-protection. In fitness terms, the effect of making a gratuitous gift and gratuitously accepting an injury works out to the same thing. Whether I donated my meal or accepted its theft, the net effect is one meal transferred from my column to that of another.

It is hard initially to see how such altruism could be a successful hereditary trait. Those who practice it (and the genes that dispose to that practice) would be less likely to have descendants than those that benefited from that altruism. Nevertheless, altruistic behavior is widespread in biological realms. Evolutionary theory has developed a robust suite of explanations for it. To

---

[25] See our discussion of intercession in Section 2.4.2.

situate those explanations in the wider theological perspective, it is helpful to lay out three interpretive stages. We could picture this as an extension ladder with three sections, each of those sections with some individual rungs or steps.

The first section has two distinct rungs. The lower rung accounts for altruistic behavior in terms of kin selection: one gives up a benefit to close relatives, whose well-being will advance your common genes equally well. Parents who sacrifice for their children (or judiciously for siblings, nieces, and nephews) enhance their success in leaving genetic descendants. The second rung accounts for additional "selfless" behavior as strictly reciprocal altruism. Within a setting where one can keep track of interactions with others, one gifts benefits to those who will reliably gift benefits back. Such altruism is a kind of "bank account" self-interest, where over time one ideally gains in return exactly as much as one gives (if not more). The gifts are more like loans. For this first sector of explanation, the precondition for altruism is either a close kinship relation or a familiar face, an identity that allows for intuitive bookkeeping of specific deposits and withdrawals.

All evolutionary biologists recognize the reality of these dynamics. But they are not sufficient to account for all observed behavior. The second section of our ladder requires us to mix in elements with a large cultural component and so of particular relevance to the human case. This section also has two rungs. The first rung is called indirect altruism. This kind of altruism extends to those in groups too large for the memory bookkeeping of reciprocal altruism to be sufficient. Indirect altruism expands to include an extensive network of nonkin in a kind of cultural family. Altruism is practiced now even between those who may have never before encountered each other in the past and may not encounter each other again, on the basis of social markers of belonging to the same network or group. For reciprocal altruism, it is necessary to remember the individual identity of a regular partner – a face. In indirect altruism, it is a name, a reputation attached to membership in a group, that is the ticket. One practices altruism toward those with the identifiers and regard of your group, in the expectation that others with the same markers and regard will do the same to you. This is ultimately about trust in the community more than the individual.

Explanation of this sort becomes more controversial when we move to a second rung. This is the point at which indirect altruism blends over into what is called group selection or multilevel selection. Two prominent figures in current evolutionary thought – E. O. Wilson and Martin Nowak – have become part of a minority party of scientists willing to directly defend this view.[26] They view groups as units of selection and the development of

---

[26] See this article and the vehement criticism of it (Nowak, Tarnita, and Wilson 2010).

altruistic members within a group as a structural variation that make the group more successful. Individuals sacrifice their fitness for the benefit of the group to which they belong. Such behaviors survive because groups with altruistic members out-survive groups without them. The soldier who sacrifices their life for their country, the single person who devotes themselves to care for the poor as a religious vocation – these people make sense not just as burnishing a reputation to gain a payoff for their genetic kin but as actual assets to the group that would not survive without them.[27]

This is not an esoteric argument. The transition from life in small, kin-and-clan-defined bodies to larger communities is crucial in human history, critical to shaping the nature of our humanity. Wherever they may stand on the debate just mentioned, scholars largely agree that religion was a prominent feature in this transition. Most theories stress the rise of "high gods," often monotheistic-like solitary deities above all others, as the referent for moral authority and enforcement: the one who "sees and judges all" even when the community has become too large for the reciprocal, intuitive bookkeeping of small groups (Norenzayan 2013). Described historically as a class, divine beings are not typically either paragons of goodness or all-powerful (effectively unrivaled by other powers). The monotheistic God, or a more monotheistic-like God, is definitely both of these. As such, God is particularly well suited for the task of overseeing a group whose interactions have grown too complex to be tracked by any participant.

Somewhere in our cultural development, humanity crossed a crucial boundary and became "eusocial." This biological category refers to a very small number of species (the best-known others being the eusocial insects, varieties of wasps, bees, and ants). These live in large, intergenerational, highly cooperative colonies, practicing an extensive division of labor, and high levels of altruism, by which colonies become a kind of superorganism (Hölldobler and Wilson 2009; Wilson 2012). Eusociality has arisen very rarely (ten–twenty times in evolutionary history) but has been enormously successful when achieved (2 percent of insect species; the eusocial insects account for 80 percent of insect biomass) (Lehrer 2012). Humanity's path to this end had to be very different from that of the eusocial insects, through culture rather than instinct. But a fundamental similarity is that both paths dramatically loosened the centrality of close kinship for community and both grew through between-group competition. As I will suggest further on, axial age religion generally and monotheism specifically seem to have been key to this phase transition in human development and forgiveness integral to monotheism's role.

---

[27] David Sloan Wilson, who has teamed with E. O. Wilson in defense of these same ideas, has developed this aspect of the question most extensively. See Wilson 2003, 2015.

Finally, there is a third section of our interpretive "ladder," the one that explicitly goes beyond what any form of biological theory would encompass. The understanding of altruism is sharpened to go beyond a descriptive term for an interaction where one participant pays a fitness cost and another gains it (a description that prescinds from any consideration of motivation, as is appropriate for a term applied across the entire biological realm). Instead, altruism is taken as a form of costly "cooperation in which an individual is motivated by good will or love for another (or others)" (Coakley 2013: 5). Some might call this true altruism, where the loss to the actor and the benefit to the recipient is the realized *purpose* of the action. The good to others (individual or group) is not only the effect of the action but also the principal reason for it.

This motivated altruism encompasses explicitly religious activity undertaken in light of a reward that does not figure at all in purely biological estimation: eternal life, communion with God, holiness, spiritual joy, and love of neighbor. We are now in the realm of theological accounts as given by the monotheistic traditions. Naturalistic accounts cannot credit these as having any objective content in their own terms. What is striking is that such naturalistic accounts differ so wildly with each other over the empirical significance and value of these religious convictions in human development (or even in contemporary life). At the one end of the spectrum, some regard such religious content as cognitive deadwood, useless byproducts of beneficial mental functions, that have been nothing but a drag on human function.[28] But on the other end, larger numbers, particularly among the cognitive scientists who study religion most carefully, think the prodigal investment of time and energy in religious ideation and practice had a commensurate functional adaptive value for human life. Specifically, these were of massive importance in the breakthrough to human eusociality (and so to large-scale human culture itself). Nor is it obvious to such researchers that such religion was needed only in that transition and does not continue to play a similar role in the continuation of human culture.[29] In perspectives like these, there is a significant convergence with theological ones.

Last of all, we can note an ultimate rung of explanation: God's practice of altruism toward creation. The gift of creation is one with no conceivable "survival" reward, a pure donation to the good and existence of the other as the other. From this perspective, the monotheistic one, we would "descend" through the various ranges of altruism/forgiveness that we have just treated as

---

[28] See the discussion of spandrels in Atran 2002: 43–45.

[29] An advocate of this approach is David Sloan Wilson. See Wilson 2019.

a pyramid of empirical accounts and see each in its own way as an image of that underlying donation.

3.3 Forgiveness and Cooperation

Recent research on mathematical principles that guide evolution, particularly the work of Martin Nowak, has connected altruism and forgiveness even more directly (Nowak 2006). The general thrust of this research suggests that cooperation drives evolution, no less than the role of selective competition. Nowak's argument is that the altruism described in the first two sections of our explanatory ladder provides the essential wiring for that cooperation. In this section, I explain how forgiveness is key to that cooperation.

Nowak argues that in the biological realm the forms of altruism we discussed lead to intensive symbiotic relations among organisms, even to their cooperative merger into communities that become, in fact, new organisms. This cooperation is a balance of competition and symbiotic trust. In the human sphere, reciprocal altruism involves personal trust toward an individual whose record and character one tracks by immediate observation. Indirect or reputational altruism involves a wider trust in a network of relations, in the spirit and distinguishing marks that bind the group. No one, and no group, can survive if that trust is constantly and completely betrayed. They cannot survive if that trust is never ventured to begin with or, as we will see, if it is never healed through forgiveness after being broken.

Nowak's special contribution comes at the intersection of game theory and evolutionary thought. He has focused on the "prisoner's dilemma" and its relevance to the evolution of cooperation (Nowak and Highfield 2011: chapter zero). The dilemma is a staple of game theory.

It pictures a stylized case in which two criminals are arrested for their joint crime and interrogated separately. If both insist on their innocence, they may both go free. If one turns against the other, the defector will receive the lighter sentence and the non-defector the longer sentence. If both turn against the other, each receives the maximum sentence. In basic terms, cooperation yields the best outcome for each, while being the lone defector produces the second-best possible outcome (for the defector alone), and mutual incrimination yields the worst outcome for both. The dilemma stems from the fact that the best course of action depends on the anticipated choice of the other party.

The relevance of this for evolutionary theory arises when it is considered as a repeated rather than one-time dilemma. The same two partners "play" again and again, not with the identical partner, but paired randomly with others in a pool of agents. The "cooperate or defect" choice is repeated, with each round yielding a graduated payoff (the most to each partner if both cooperated, the next best payoff if you are the defector and your partner cooperates, and the least to each if both defect). Such versions of the game allow different strategies to be tested, in "tournaments" of competing computer programs. To condense some fascinating complexity, initially, the winning strategy appeared to be a simple and familiar one: "tit for tat" (Nowak and Highfield 2011: chapter one). When one's partner cooperated in the last move, you do the same in the next. If they defected, you "punish" them by defecting on your next move. An "eye for an eye," a meticulously unforgiving strategy, seems to be the biological imperative.

But when the game was adjusted to better reflect the real world, this changed. In the real world, it is not always possible to know perfectly whether someone has cooperated or not, or whether they intended to defect or not, or whether they repent of defecting. Limits to knowledge and errors in perception are always present. When realistic recognition of such "noise" in the system was factored in, another program was the clear winner: "generous tit for tat" (Nowak and Highfield 2011: 33–37). A great liability of the "tit-for-tat" strategy is that once one side defects, even if this is done by mistake or one later wishes to have chosen otherwise, the strategy dictates that both sides will mirror each other's negation in a permanent death spiral. This locks them in a low payoff mode. Generous tit for tat practices random acts of non-retaliation, on occasion responding to defection with cooperation in the next round. A "player" willing to episodically practice forgiveness, to act without holding the immediate past behavior of the other against them, will statistically obtain a much better outcome for their own benefit (and possibly for their partner participants as well).

Nowak and his colleagues discovered that in this computer simulation world, the more realistic they were, the less their world settled into any static equilibrium (Nowak and Highfield 2011: 36, 48). The system as a whole went through cyclic phases, favoring different strategies, and the overall or cumulative "winner" was not dominant in all phases. Sometimes "selfish" programs rose to near dominance, before being undermined by their death spiral tendencies. As more "generous" programs gained success, it became possible for them to be outcompeted by even more forgiving programs that could take advantage, at least for a while, of a friendly environment in which most of their potential partners were ready cooperators. But, at that point, the fortunes of more selfish strategies could revive in a rich climate of "suckers." There was an unresolved tension between a race to the bottom and a parallel race to the top.

This approach offers a novel perspective on our topic, quantifying a stripped-down paradigm for forgiveness. The "injury" is the defection of the partner, for which the "just" and the narrowly selfish evolutionary response would appear to be an eye for an eye. However, the successful strategy (successful in the sense of being most prevalent over time but never permanently established) is one that incorporates a principle of non-retaliation. There are distinct limits on forgiveness in this model. In generous tit for tat, forgiveness is applied rather indiscriminately within the system. Its total frequency is restrained. Forgiveness is a seasoning, not a constant. Too little or too much can be destructive for individuals and for groups. But its complete absence is inevitably destructive.

Forgiveness as the most effective strategy may seem a contradiction in terms. If one undertakes it with this intention, is it actually forgiveness? Clearly, forgiveness must make sense at the individual level at which it actually takes place. But the key takeaway here is that forgiveness has a systemic role, where the health of individual organisms interlocks with the health of their communities. Groups that foster forgiveness among their members can be healthier than those that do not.

In certain respects, this mirrors the spiritual dynamics of forgiveness. One can focus on the benefits, both spiritual and practical, that may flow to the forgiver (release from bitterness, freedom for new life, and healing) or to the offender and the relative balance between them. Or one can see the process as part of an economy of abundance, in the sense that forgiveness, like the more generous strategies in Nowak's simulations, improves the outcomes for both forgiver and forgiven and even for others belonging to the same community. In social terms, forgiveness is not a zero-sum game.[30]

This gives us an interesting perspective on the default context for human forgiveness. We see how others may have a profound investment in the practice or non-practice of forgiveness between the primary parties. In the last section, we discussed this in terms of intercession, forgiveness granted for the sake of someone other than the primary parties. Now we find that in very concrete terms, it can be the entire community that is the "intercessor." We can see that there is a reverse dynamic as well. I might be less forgiving of someone's offense against me in light of the past betrayal by someone *else*. I may become more likely to forgive a member of my group because in the past other members have been forgiving to me. When the scope widens in this way, forgiveness becomes to some extent a function of the state of a web of relations beyond that of the immediate parties. It belongs to a wider good.

Our societies incorporate many aspects of the excess we have been discussing. We build in structural reset features for those who have been "defectors" in their social engagements: bankruptcy regulations for financial defaulters,

---

[30] For more on this general idea, see Wright 2001.

different standards for first as opposed to repeat offenders, and judicial sanctions distinguishing juveniles from adults. Such systemic forms of forgiveness seek to serve the group as a whole, to avoid negative feedback spirals, and to maximize the collective good. They concretely embody the generous dimension of "generous tit for tat." But these structural resets draw on a finite reservoir of social capital, the spontaneous trust and cooperative behavior circulating in the community at large, based on an expectation that others will return the same trust and cooperation. If that capital falls below a certain level, all will suffer dramatically. Just as at the individual level we look for repentance to typically precede forgiveness, at the collective level, we look for a more diffuse but real benefit to come to the community in the wake of systemic forms of forgiveness.

3.4 The Excess of Universal Forgiveness

There is a necessary place for cooperation in the purely biological story and for forgiveness as an aspect of the altruism that fuels that cooperation. Such forgiveness may not apply in every *event*, even as it extends to *everyone* within a widening horizon. But religions (as illustrated with our Buddhist example), and monotheisms, more specifically, do not seem to be in the business of advocating only probabilistic and strategic forgiveness of the sort we have just described. They teach a universal and unrestrained version, notable for its excess.

Yet, monotheisms do fit well with the pattern we have described in one respect. We noted that for monotheisms, forgiveness is a virtue that applies particularly to those with a future together. This appears empirically true, in that the practice of forgiveness flourishes among those who believe they have a social future together. In the light of our biological discussion, we could also say that without the practice of forgiveness, communities and their members do not have a cooperative future together.

Monotheisms understand this future ultimately in eschatological terms. An interesting note from Nowak's studies is that the flux in his system sometimes verged toward an extremely high level of cooperation and forgiveness. The meek do (temporarily) inherit the earth, practicing an "excess" where reciprocity and proactive non-retaliation lead to a mutual abundance before this situation regresses in the opposite direction. The eschatological vision is that this impermanent tendency can be deepened and stabilized and that this is the divine aim. That fruitful circle (as opposed to the vicious one of reciprocal betrayal) can rachet up to a point where everyone's willingness to forgive is constitutive of an order or community in which no one any longer needs to be forgiven. The hope for forgiveness as a universal feature stakes out this final horizon.

Our quick overview of an evolutionary perspective raises the possibility that the ideal of a truly universal "excess" in forgiveness is only a veneer, a façade that stands in truth only for a preferential generosity toward those in one's own religious group. And there certainly are strong tendencies in the monotheistic faiths to apply those principles first and most strongly among the faithful. Some of the injunctions now routinely seen as universal in scope might initially have referred primarily to the circle of co-believers. The Lord's Prayer frames its request to God to "forgive us our sins as we forgive those who sin against us" in a form consistent with indirect altruism, where forgiveness defines an in-group network. The practice of forgiveness with each other is a kind of intercession to God on our own behalf.

The objection that the teaching of universal forgiveness serves only the selfishness of the religious group ignores the fact that "selfishness" on such a community level already marked an extraordinary transformation. The first great barrier to be breached in the expansion of human cooperation and culture was the kin envelope. In advancing a universal ethic, specifically a universal diagnosis of the need and the application of forgiveness, monotheisms played a key role in widening the circle from family and immediate clan to a new "all," a network or group of a size where kinship and facial recognition were no longer sufficient guides. Far from a mere proxy for the selfishness of the *existing* group, the religious horizon opened scope for a dramatic expansion in the circle of mutual regard toward a vastly larger, not-yet-constituted group. An evolutionary view suggests it was precisely the excess in the religious scope of forgiveness, for instance, that helped shift the biological goalposts toward human eusociality, the extraordinary breakthrough we discussed previously.

The religious teaching of forgiveness thematizes the components Nowak describes as mathematical and biological constants in all life. Religion itself was an enabling means by which they could be instantiated in the transition to the eusociality of human culture (Henrich 2020: 146–51). Those unrelated and unfamiliar ones who belonged to this wider network became cultural "kin" by becoming part of the new, religiously defined unity. Too large to be integrated by individual memory or comprehension, the group was united by one maker, one lawgiver, one whose perspective encompassed and judged all. Leaving vengeance to the Lord meant to practice forgiveness within this community. The limited scale of community defined by close biological relation was expanded by religious "adoption" of others.

Monotheism's universal reference may regularly have been "stepped down" in practical application, from an absolute scope to one that included less than all humanity. It still represented a quantum expansion of the prior scale of both imagined and actualized human solidarity. The vision of forgiveness without boundaries spread this dynamic into operation within groups wider than kin, even though the relevant universe remained a group (now a much larger group) among other groups. To forgive someone you had never met, because of their commonality with you in this new scale of community, was to forgive "all" with a newly universal scope. Monotheisms understood themselves to be universal in a manner commensurate with the scope of the God they worshipped. Thus, whether they were explicitly conversionist (as Christianity and Islam) or not (as with Judaism), the current boundaries of intergroup competition were not fixed, and the members of other groups were the objects of God's concern and potential members of the "home" group, now or eschatologically.

Evolutionary accounts of religion argue that altruistic religious practices are a kind of "costly signaling" (Irons 2001). The evident harm from such behavior for an individual's reproductive fitness advertises a deep commitment to the community whose regime (fasting, poverty, and celibacy) they follow. Such signaling marks those people as very dependable community members, toward whom other community members will then readily practice proactive altruism. Even more, this costly display reinforces such practices among all others in the community and advertises the benefits of belonging to a community with such strong reciprocal expectations. Forgiveness, with the practical loss and psychological burden it imposes, plainly fits this pattern. Of course, from a different perspective "costly signaling" is simply another name for religious sincerity. Recognition that the benefits of this signal accrue to unrelated members of the larger group only underlines the fact that the explicit altruistic religious intent of the actor corresponds to its actual effect. Its "utility" actually converges with its religious understanding.

Cooperation is enhanced not only with a carrot but also with a stick. A peculiar but well-attested form of altruism is that exhibited by people who will pay a fitness cost in order to punish others who violate the expectation for fairness and reciprocity (Nowak and Highfield 2011: 223ff). That is, though individuals may be encouraged to practice proactive non-retaliation in regard to those who harm them directly, they are also encouraged to distinguish those who manifest repentance (and commitment to the convictions that ground forgiveness) from those that do not. Some discipline against those in the latter category follows. This discipline against "free riders" in the community is the flip side of the costly signaling behavior, similar in that both require the sacrifice of selfish interest and both increase the dependability of mutual support going forward. So it is notable that monotheistic religious communities historically practice forms of discipline, through sanctions up to and including expulsion form the community. This practice always holds out the hope and possibility of future forgiveness and reconciliation. But it reflects convictions that as a result of sin and evil, there are necessary exceptions to the simple universal practice of forgiveness, particularly on the level of the community.[31]

Many of the differences among monotheisms, particularly those we discussed in the last section relating to the conditions for forgiveness, can be seen as variations in response to this common problem. It is the same problem we saw in Nowak's models, the tension between the impetus toward altruistic generosity that can drive the group to higher levels of non-zero-sum cooperation and the constraints required to police the rise of defector strategies that will take advantage of the proactive altruism.[32] Only the drive toward the universal horizon can do the former, and only "in-group" boundaries and standards can do the latter. The religious ideal is continually constrained by this tension. The eusocial breakthrough created a cultural setting where there are benefits to be found for human groups that explore higher levels of generosity, as non-zero-sum communities, straining toward more universal implementation of the religious ideals.

Clearly, the Abrahamic traditions press toward a universal eschatological horizon and so toward forgiveness beyond any limit of social utility and toward an unconditional excess. The internal dynamic of these universals was to become more truly universal. This is evident in elements within each tradition that offer an explicit internal critique against restricting forgiveness to the group itself. So, for instance, the parable of the good Samaritan teaches the practice of this beneficence in a pre-reciprocal manner toward those who are outside the religious and ethnic community. So do Jewish teachings in regard to the stranger and sojourner or Muslim teachings about other "peoples of the book."

The exhortation to forgive your *enemies* underlines this point in the strongest way, pointing specifically to those who pose the greatest threat to an "in group." Instances and ideals of forgiveness with such radical scope look toward a reconciliation in which competing groups (the groups whose competition itself encouraged the development of forgiveness as a feature within ever larger groups) unite. It is a constant of eschatological expectation that all of humanity will become one community. The eschatological dimension of this teaching goes far beyond an understanding of forgiveness as simply part of the warp and woof of viable community life among a group with strong religious identity markers, important as religion may be in that connection in human history.

---

[31] This point is made very helpful by D. S. Wilson. He points out that facile dismissals of the "hypocrisy" of religious teachings about forgiveness do not take into account the nuance with which they are always applied and explained. See chapter six, "Forgiveness as a Complex Adaptation," in Wilson 2003.

[32] See Section 3.3

Monotheism's universal horizon pulled humans from a narrow kin and clan circle into truly eusocial communities, larger than any whose specific members can be cataloged in one brain. This dramatically expanded the functional boundary of the "all" in humanity. The competition that figures in this expansion was never limited to that between human groups. It included human struggles to find sustainable livelihoods in relation to the nonhuman communities of microbes, vegetation, and animals that surrounded them. Cooperation, and the forgiveness integral to it, raises the fitness of human groups to flourish in the wider world.

As monotheistic religion played a key role in humanity's first eusocial breakthrough, so the "excess" dimension in its approach to forgiveness may figure in a second, of equal moment.

This breakthrough would correspond to monotheisms' explicit theoretical expectation for the relevant group to become humanity as a whole. David Sloan Wilson recognizes that religion was integral to the earlier eusocial transition. He suggests that his own secular, evolutionary perspective converges with the monotheistic universal imagination in one profound conclusion. This is the assertion "that the concept of 'organism' has a movable boundary, which must be expanded to solve the problems of our age" (Wilson 2019: 14–15). The boundary that shifted to make human groups effectively into complex organisms, rising and falling in part on the strength of their inner relations, can move again, to bring all of humanity, and its necessary biosphere, within that boundary.

Conclusion

Like a crude radiological scan, our review of forgiveness within monotheism shows up major structural components. Our first section illustrated the distinctive orientation of this forgiveness toward the future of the personal and social worlds. Our second section highlighted a cross section of the practice of forgiveness, from the diagnosis of transgression through the response of confession, repentance, intercession, and reconciliation. The last section illuminated the role that the eschatological and universal "excess" in monotheistic visions of forgiveness has played in human cultural development.

References

ABC News. 2015. "Dylan Roof hears victims' families speak at first court appearance: 'I forgive you'," accessed December 3, 2020. https://abcnews .go.com/US/dylann-roofhearsvictims-families-speak-1st-court/story? id=31896001.

Asín Palacios, Miguel, and Harold Sunderland. 1968. *Islam and the divine comedy* (Cass: London).

Assmann, Jan. 2010. *The price of monotheism* (Stanford University Press: Stanford).

Atran, Scott. 2002. *In gods we trust: The evolutionary landscape of religion* (Oxford University Press: Oxford; New York).

Ayoub, Mahmoud. 1978. *Redemptive suffering in Islām: A study of the devotional aspects of "Āshūrā" in twelver Shī'ism* (Mouton: The Hague).

Bailey, Kenneth E. 1998. *"The pursuing father," Christianity Today* 42: 34–36.

Bellah, Robert N. 2011. *Religion in human evolution: From the Paleolithic to the Axial Age* (Belknap Press of Harvard University Press: Cambridge, MA).

Bettencourt, Megan Feldman. 2015. *Triumph of the heart: Forgiveness in an unforgiving world* (Hudson Street Press: New York).

Brown, Jonathan A. C. 2016. "Sin, forgiveness, and reconciliation: A Muslim perspective" in Lucinda Mosher and David Marshall (eds.), *Sin, forgiveness, and reconciliation: Christian and Muslim perspectives* (Georgetown University Press: Washington, DC).

Chen, Ying, Sion Kim Harris, Everett L. Worthington, and Tyler J. VanderWeele. 2019. "Religiously or spiritually motivated forgiveness and subsequent health and well-being among young adults: An outcome-wide analysis," *The Journal of Positive Psychology* 14: 649–58.

Coakley, Sarah. 2013. "Introduction" in M. A. Nowak and Sarah Coakley (eds.), *Evolution, games, and God: The principle of cooperation* (Harvard University Press: Cambridge, MA).

Freud, Sigmund, and Joyce Crick. 2002. *The joke and its relation to the unconscious* (Penguin: London; New York).

Glassé, Cyril. 1989. *The concise encyclopedia of Islam* (Harper & Row: San Francisco).

Globe Newspaper. 2002. *Betrayal: The crisis in the Catholic Church* (Little, Brown: Boston).

Gregg, Robert C. 2015. *Shared stories, rival tellings: Early encounters of Jews, Christians, and Muslims* (Oxford University Press: Oxford; New York).

Gyatso, Tenzin. 2009. *For the benefit of all beings: A commentary on the way of the Bodhisattva* (Shambhala: Boston).

Heim, S. Mark. 1995. *Salvations: Truth and difference in religion* (Orbis Books: Maryknoll).

2006. *Saved from sacrifice: A theology of the cross* (William B. Eerdmans: Grand Rapids).

2014. "Religion in the perspective of 'big history'," *Harvard Theological Review* 107: 114–26.

2019. *Crucified wisdom: Theological reflection on Christ and the Bodhisattva* (Fordham University Press: New York).

Henrich, Joseph Patrick. 2020. *The WEIRDest people in the world: How the west became psychologically peculiar and particularly prosperous* (Farrar, Straus and Giroux: New York).

Hölldobler, Bert, and Edward O. Wilson. 2009. *The superorganism: The beauty, elegance, and strangeness of insect societies* (W. W. Norton: New York).

"The Imam and the Pastor." 2008. 39:20 FLT Films.

Irons, William G. 2001. "Religion as a hard-to-fake sign of commitment" in R. Nesse (ed.), *Evolution and the capacity for commitment* (Russell Sage Foundation: New York).

Karkkainen, Velli-Matti. 2016. "Sin, forgiveness, and reconciliation: A Christian perspective" in Lucinda Mosher, David Marshall, and ProQuest (Firm) (eds.), *Sin, forgiveness, and reconciliation: Christian and Muslim perspectives: A record of the Thirteenth Building Bridges Seminar hosted by Georgetown University Washington, District of Columbia & Warrenton, Virginia April 27–30, 2014* (Georgetown University Press: Washington, DC).

Keown, Damien. 2013. *Buddhism: A very short introduction* (Oxford University Press: Oxford).

Kraybill, Donald B., Steven M. Nolt, and David Weaver-Zercher. 2007. *Amish grace: How forgiveness transcended tragedy* (Jossey-Bass: San Francisco).

Lange, Christian. 2016. *Paradise and hell in Islamic traditions* (Cambridge University Press: New York).

Lehrer, Jonah. 2012. "Kin and kind: A fight about the genetics of altruism," *The New Yorker*. www.newyorker.com/magazine/2012/03/05/kin-kind.

Liechty, Joseph. 2006. "Putting forgiveness in its place: The dynamics of reconciliation" in Joseph Liechty and David Tombs (eds.), *Explorations in reconciliation: New directions in theology* (Routledge: London).

Luskin, Frederic. 2020. "Forgive for good," accessed September 19, 2020. https://learningtoforgive.com/9-steps/.

Moltmann, Jürgen, and Jürgen Moltmann. 1980. *Experiences of God* (Fortress Press: Philadelphia).

Muslim. 2020. "Sahih Muslim," accessed May 13, 2021. https://quranx.com/Hadith/Muslim/USC-MSA/Book-37/Hadith–6622.

Nasr, Seyyed Hossein, Caner K. Dagli, Maria Massi Dakake, Joseph E. B. Lumbard, and Mohammed Rustom. 2015. *The study Quran: A new translation and commentary* (HarperOne, An Imprint of HarperCollins: New York).

Norenzayan, Ara. 2013. *Big Gods: How religion transformed cooperation and conflict* (Princeton University Press: Princeton).

Nowak, M. A., and Roger Highfield. 2011. *Supercooperators: Altruism, evolution, and why we need each other to succeed* (Free Press: New York).

Nowak, Martin A. 2006. "Five rules for the evolution of cooperation," *Science* 31(5805): 1560–63.

Nowak, Martin A., Corina E. Tarnita, and Edmund O. Wilson. 2010. "The evolution of eusociality," *Nature* 466: 1057–62.

Palmer, Martin, Jay Ramsay, and Man-Ho Kwok. 2009. *The Kuan Yin chronicles: The myths and prophecies of the Chinese Goddess of compassion* (Hampton Roads: Charlottesville).

Reeves, Gene. 2008. *The Lotus Sutra: A contemporary translation of a Buddhist classic* (Wisdom: Boston).

Śāntideva, Kate Crosby, and Andrew Skilton. 1996. "The Bodhicaryávatára," *The World's Classics*: xlviii, 191.

Śāntideva, Vesna A. Wallace, and B. Alan Wallace. 1997. *A guide to the Bodhisattva way of life (Bodhicaryávatára)* (Snow Lion: Ithaca).

Sartiprak, Zeki. 2011. "Reconciliation: An Islamic theological approach" in Reimund Bieringer and David J. Bolton (eds.), *Reconciliation in interfaith perspective* (Peeters: Leuven).

Schimmel, Solomon. 2002. *Wounds not healed by time: The power of repentance and forgiveness* (Oxford University Press: Oxford; New York).

Schwartz, Regina M. 1997. *The curse of Cain: The violent legacy of monotheism* (University of Chicago Press: Chicago).

Shah-Kazemi, Reza. 2019. "Forgiveness in Islam: From prophetic practice to divine principle" in Stephen Hance (ed.), *Forgiveness in practice* (Jessica Kingsley: London; Philadelphia).

Toussaint, Loren, Everett Worthington, David R. Williams, and SpringerLink (Online service). *Forgiveness and Health Scientific Evidence and Theories Relating Forgiveness to Better Health*. 2015. https://yale.idm.oclc.org/login?URL=http://dx.doi.org/10.1007/978-94-017-9993-5.

Tucker, Jeritt R., Rachel L. Bitman, Nathaniel G. Wade, and Marilyn A. Cornish. 2015. "Defining forgiveness: Historical roots, contemporary research, and key considerations for health outcomes" in Everett L. Worthington, Loren L. Toussaint, and David R. Williams (eds.), *Forgiveness and health scientific evidence and theories relating forgiveness to better health* (Springer: Dordrecht).

Valea, Ernest. 2009. *The Buddha and the Christ – Reciprocal views* (Booksurge).

Van Ness, Daniel W., and Karen Heetderks Strong. 2010. *Restoring justice: An introduction to restorative justice* (LexisNexis: Anderson: New Providence).

VanderWeele, Tyler J. 2018. "Is forgiveness a public health issue?," *American Journal of Public Health* 108: 189–90.

Volf, Miroslav. 1996. *Exclusion and embrace: A theological exploration of identity, otherness, and reconciliation* (Abingdon Press: Nashville).

2005. *Free of charge: Giving and forgiving in a culture stripped of grace: The Archbishop's official 2006 Lent book* (Zondervan: Grand Rapids).

Wade, N. G., Everett L. Worthington, and J. Meyer. 2005. "But do they work? Meta-analysis of group interventions to promote forgiveness" in Everett L. Worthington (ed.), *Handbook of forgiveness* (Routledge: New York).

Wiesenthal, Simon, Harry J. Cargas, and Bonny V. Fetterman. 1998. *The sunflower: On the possibilities and limits of forgiveness* (Schocken Books: New York).

Wilson, David Sloan. 2003. *Darwin's cathedral: Evolution, religion, and the nature of society* (University of Chicago Press: Chicago; London).

2015. *Does altruism exist? Culture, genes, and the welfare of others* (Yale University Press: Templeton Press: New Haven; London).

2019. *This view of life: Completing the Darwinian revolution* (Pantheon Books: New York).

Wilson, Edward O. 2012. *The social conquest of earth* (Liveright: New York).

Wright, Robert. 2001. *NonZero: The logic of human destiny* (Vintage Books: New York).

Yancey, Philip. 1997. *What's so amazing about grace?* (Zondervan: Grand Rapids).

Yusuf, Hamza. 2015. "Death, dying, and the afterlife in the Quran" in Seyyed Hossein Nasr, Caner K. Dagli, Maria Massi Dakake, Joseph E. B. Lumbard, and Mohammed Rustom (eds.), *The study Quran: A new translation and commentary* (HarperOne, An Imprint of HarperCollins: New York).

Acknowledgments

In regard to Islam, I want to express thanks to Reza Shah-Kazemi for the use of some unpublished material as well as for his written work and to Abdul-Rehman Malik for conversation and suggestions relative to this Element. In regard to Judaism, I likewise am indebted to Sol Schimmel and Nehemia Polen for the learning gained in our colleagueship in the joint programs of Hebrew College and Andover Newton Theological School over a number of years. I am especially grateful to Professor Polen for the courses that we taught together over that time. My thanks go also to Dick Ransom, whose extraordinary teaching program at First Baptist Church in Newton, MA, has gone deeply into texts from all three traditions. Needless to say, none of these are responsible for misunderstandings or errors in my work that may remain.

Cambridge Elements $\equiv$

Religion and Monotheism

Paul K. Moser

Loyola University Chicago

Paul K. Moser is a professor of philosophy at Loyola University Chicago. He is the author of *Understanding Religious Experience, The God Relationship, The Elusive God* (winner of national book award from the Jesuit Honor Society), *The Evidence for God, The Severity of God, Knowledge and Evidence* (all Cambridge University Press), and *Philosophy after Objectivity* (Oxford University Press); coauthor of *Theory of Knowledge* (Oxford University Press); editor of *Jesus and Philosophy* (Cambridge University Press) and *The Oxford Handbook of Epistemology* (Oxford University Press); and coeditor of *The Wisdom of the Christian Faith* (Cambridge University Press). He is the coeditor with Chad Meister of the book series *Cambridge Studies in Religion, Philosophy, and Society.*

Chad Meister

Bethel University

Chad Meister is a professor of philosophy and theology and department chair at Bethel College. He is the author of *Introducing Philosophy of Religion* (Routledge, 2009), *Christian Thought: A Historical Introduction*, 2nd edition (Routledge, 2017), and *Evil: A Guide for the Perplexed*, 2nd edition (Bloomsbury, 2018). He has edited or coedited the following: *The Oxford Handbook of Religious Diversity* (Oxford University Press, 2010); *Debating Christian Theism* (Oxford University Press, 2011); with Paul Moser, *The Cambridge Companion to the Problem of Evil* (Cambridge University Press, 2017); and with Charles Taliaferro, *The History of Evil* (Routledge 2018, in six volumes).

About the Series

This Element series publishes original concise volumes on monotheism and its significance. Monotheism as occupied inquirers since the time of the Biblical patriarch, and it continues to attract interdisciplinary academic work today. Engaging, current, and concise, the Elements benefit teachers, researchers, and advanced students in religious studies, biblical studies, theology, philosophy of religion, and related fields.

Cambridge Elements ☰

Religion and Monotheism

Printed in the United States
by Baker & Taylor Publisher Services